A Brief History of the World
Part II

Professor Peter N. Stearns

THE TEACHING COMPANY ®

PUBLISHED BY:

THE TEACHING COMPANY
4151 Lafayette Center Drive, Suite 100
Chantilly, Virginia 20151-1232
1-800-TEACH-12
Fax 703-378-3819
www.teach12.com

ISBN 978-1-59803-327-4

Peter N. Stearns, Ph.D.
Provost and Professor of History, George Mason University

Peter N. Stearns is Provost and Professor of History at George Mason University, where he annually teaches a world history course for undergraduates. He previously taught at the University of Chicago, Rutgers, and Carnegie Mellon and was trained at Harvard University. While at Carnegie Mellon, Professor Stearns won the Smith award for teaching in the College of Humanities and Social Sciences and the Spencer award for excellence in university teaching. He has worked extensively for the Advanced Placement program and chaired the committee that devised and implemented the AP world history course (1996–2006). Professor Stearns was Vice President of the American Historical Association, heading its Teaching Division from 1995 to 1998. He also founded and still edits the *Journal of Social History*.

Trained in European social history, Professor Stearns has authored a wide array of books and articles (on both Europe and the United States) on such subjects as emotions, childrearing, dieting and obesity, old age, and work. He has also written widely in world history, authoring two textbooks that have gone through multiple editions. He edited the sixth edition of the *Encyclopedia of World History* and is currently editing an *Encyclopedia of Modern World History*. He has written several thematic studies in world history, including *The Industrial Revolution in World History* (2nd ed., Westview, 1998), *Gender in World History* (2nd ed., Routledge, 2006), *Consumerism in World History* (2nd ed., Routledge, 2006), *Western Civilization in World History* (Routledge, 2003), and *Childhood in World History* (Routledge, 2005). His book *Global Outrage: The Evolution and Impact of World Opinion* (OneWorld) appeared in 2005, and his current interest in using history to understand contemporary patterns of behavior is illustrated in *American Fear* (Routledge, 2006).

Professor Stearns was "converted" to world history more than two decades ago and has taught it annually since then, first at Carnegie Mellon and currently at George Mason. He believes that the framework of world history allows him to learn a great deal about the world without degenerating into random detail and helps his students to better understand the past and the present.

Table of Contents

A Brief History of the World
Part II

A Brief History of the World

Scope:

This course presents some of the highlights of the world historical approach to the past, suggesting major changes in the framework of the human experience, from the rise of agriculture to the present day. The lectures cover the emergence of distinct major societies as they deal with common problems but generate quite different institutional and cultural approaches. The course also discusses key changes in belief systems—the emergence and spread of the great world religions, for example—as well as alterations in trading patterns and basic shifts in technology, exploring why some societies reacted differently to technological change than others.

Throughout the course, we will look at many parts of the world, including those clustered into shared civilizations. East Asia, South Asia, the Middle East, and the Mediterranean loom large from the start. Sub-Saharan Africa, where the human species originated, has also played a great role in world history, as ultimately has northern Europe, including Russia. The Americas offer an important variant until their incorporation in global patterns from 1492 onward. Central Asia maintained a distinct position in world history until the 16th century.

World history divides into a limited number of time periods, defined in terms of dominant themes. The rise of agriculture requires a discussion of pre-agricultural patterns. Following agriculture came, in several places, the advent of civilization as a form of human organization. The classical period in world history draws attention to China, India, Persia, and the Mediterranean, when the expansion and integration of these large societies dominated over a millennium of human history. The collapse of the classical empires ushered in a vital postclassical period, when emphasis shifted to religion but also to more ambitious patterns of interregional trade. It was in this postclassical period (500–1500 CE) that the emphasis of major societies shifted from separate development to greater interaction and even deliberate imitation. The early modern period highlights a renewed capacity for empire, the inclusion of the Americas in global systems, and—though this must be handled with a bit of care—the rise of Western Europe. What some historians call the "Long 19th

Century"—1750 or so to 1914—was dominated by Western industrialization and its economic, military, and cultural impact on, literally, the entire world. Finally, the Contemporary period in world history, after World War I, features a bewildering variety of themes that must be sorted out, with emphasis among other things on the relative decline of the West, the huge surge in human population, and the potential for greater globalization.

World history highlights a number of major regions, but it avoids simply examining one area after another—"if it's Tuesday, this must be Latin America"—by making careful comparisons and focusing on interregional contacts. The discipline emphasizes a number of key time periods (though not an indefinite number), defined in terms of basic changes in the ways many societies operated, whether the change was in an economic system—industrialization, for example— or a cultural system, as seen, for example, in the emergence of vigorous missionary religions.

World history also embraces two common themes. First, and most obviously, is the eternal tension between change and continuity—the stuff of history as a discipline. Particularly once the classical traditions are defined, world history can be seen in terms of new forces being met and interpreted by established cultural and institutional systems. Of course, these systems change but never completely and never in exactly the same ways from one society to the next.

The second theme involves a perpetual interplay between local or regional identities, on the one hand, and the attraction or simple inevitability of wider contacts, on the other. Societies began trading at long distances several millennia ago. They received immigrants and diseases and, sometimes, ideas from distant places. But they rarely, at least willingly, simply surrendered to outside influence, and sometimes they battled fiercely against such influence in the name of established values. Over time, of course, and particularly with contemporary globalization, the pendulum shifted toward more outside influence, either willingly embraced or endured of necessity. But the tension has not ended, and assertions of regional identities can intensify precisely because the external framework is so intrusive. World history allows us to trace the main iterations of this tension and to place its current iteration in context—and even, tentatively, to talk about its future.

Lecture Thirteen
Postclassical Trade and Contacts

Scope:

The increase of interregional trade in the postclassical centuries created and reflected a number of changes. An unprecedented range of areas became involved in what we now call international trade. While still focused heavily on luxury products, the amount and variety of trade changed as well, and new consumer tastes emerged. Trade brought other changes, for example, in shipping technology, mapping, and new opportunities for travelers. New contacts promoted missionary religions but also exchanges of technologies and other systems. It is possible to interpret this surge as the basis for the steady acceleration of trade activities that would ultimately produce globalization.

Outline

I. The new range and intensity of contacts was, along with the spread of world religions, a crucial development in the postclassical period, affecting most of Asia and many parts of Africa and Europe. In this lecture, we will look at the emergence of world travelers as a byproduct of these new patterns of contact, along with the major routes and consequences of contact.

II. In the 14th century, one of the greatest world travelers was Ibn Battuta.

    A. Battuta was born in Morocco in northwestern Africa to a middle-class merchant family. He launched his travels with a pilgrimage to Mecca.

    B. In his lifetime, Battuta's travels would take him to Mecca and other parts of North Africa, the Middle East, Persia, Central Asia, India, island groups in the Indian Ocean, Southeast Asia, China, and sub-Saharan Africa.

    C. Battuta's accounts of his travels both reflected and encouraged the new range of geographical contact that was then possible.

D. He was motivated to travel by his religious faith, his desire for sexual encounters, and a massive curiosity about different places.

E. In addition to illustrating the potential for geographical expression of human curiosity, Battuta's accounts reflect other noteworthy features.

    1. He judged his destinations by the standards of Islam. He praised religious piety but deplored departures from the norm.

    2. In his one clear venture well outside Islam, his visit to China, Battuta praised Chinese society and cities, but was disoriented without the presence of an Islamic overlay.

III. Another great traveler of the postclassical period was Marco Polo, the Venetian who presumably went to China under Mongol rule and reported on what he found there.

A. We are not sure that Marco Polo actually went to China. His uncles visited China, and he may have used their accounts, along with Persian travel literature, to fabricate a version of his own travels.

B. If Marco Polo did not travel to China, other Europeans clearly did, sometimes returning via the Indian Ocean and thus encountering South, Southeast, and East Asia.

C. The European travelers differed from Ibn Battuta in one respect: they were less uncomfortable in settings outside their religious orbit.

D. Combining the cases of Ibn Battuta and Marco Polo (or Polo's uncles), we get a sense of the extent to which people visited distant places. By their accounts, these travelers spurred others to seek new trade and contact opportunities.

E. Travel in this period differed greatly from what had been possible in the earlier classical era. The travelers went farther and encountered far more different situations, and their accounts are much more consistently accurate than earlier ones. These changes reflect a different world.

IV. Let us now turn to the patterns of contact.

    A. The core route for the new pattern of contact that emerged in the postclassical period was an Indian Ocean route connecting western Asia or the Middle East with South Asia, Southeast Asia, and the Pacific coast of China.

        1. This series of routes was initially forged by Arab merchants primarily, but they were soon joined by Muslims and others from India, Southeast Asia, and elsewhere, and by a number of Persians.

        2. These routes carried a variety of goods. Particularly important were manufactured goods from China, such as silk and porcelain, and spices from Southeast Asia or India.

        3. This Asian-centered trade pattern spurred major manufacturing expansions, particularly in China. During the Song dynasty, which opened in the later-10th century, some historians have even referred to a Chinese industrial revolution.

    B. Other routes fed into the east-west contact.

        1. Two routes connected sub-Saharan Africa to this east-west trade, carrying African goods into the Middle East, North Africa, and other parts of Asia.

        2. Another feeder route developed from Scandinavia through what is now western Russia and Ukraine, passing through Kiev on its way to the Byzantine Empire and then connecting with Arab trade.

        3. Western Europe also eventually connected with this trade route as merchants from England, the Low Countries, and France traveled over land or along the Atlantic coast to the Mediterranean, the Middle East, and beyond.

V. A number of important consequences can be seen from these trading patterns.

    A. This level of interregional trade had a significant impact on internal economies, particularly the economy of China. Some areas of the world—again particularly China—began to orient part of their economic activity toward production for what we would call world markets.

B. New kinds of consumer dependence developed as well. Certain elements of the upper classes in a number of societies developed tastes for goods that could be supplied only from distant regions.

    1. As West Europeans, particularly noblemen, participated in the Crusades, they learned of the higher living standards common in Middle Eastern cities and developed a taste for that lifestyle.

    2. Postclassical Europeans found that they preferred sugar to honey and sought to acquire access to regular supplies of sugar.

    3. This kind of consumer attachment spurred shipping activities in the Mediterranean that would link Europe to Middle Eastern ports where products could be transshipped from elsewhere in Asia.

    4. Not all societies were equally susceptible to consumer needs. China, for example, needed far fewer products from the outside world than did Western Europe.

C. Another important consequence involves new levels of culture contact.

    1. A large number of words began to pass into European languages from Arabic, denoting the products (such as oranges or sugar) that were being transshipped from other parts of the world to Europe.

    2. Other kinds of cultural exchange were even more important, particularly the widespread adoption of what Europeans called the Arabic numbering system.

    3. Mathematical systems spread widely. Algebra (another Arabic word) and Arabic mathematical innovation began to spread from the Arab world to other societies, including Europe.

D. Technologies were affected by new levels of world trade in two ways: new trading activities encouraged the development of new technologies, and increased trade accelerated the transmission of technological inventions.

    1. The Arabs introduced developments in sailing ships, and, toward the end of the postclassical period, the Chinese introduced gigantic oceangoing vessels (junks).

    2. The compass was probably invented in China, but its use spread.

3. The Arabs learned about paper in their military interactions in Western China; Western Europeans learned about paper from contact with the Arabs.

E. An important consequence of new trade patterns was the growing utility that societies in Asia, Africa, and Europe found in maintaining or increasing their commitment to international activities.

VI. The postclassical period was a watershed in world history as interregional connections developed and solidified by 1000 CE onward.

   A. Many societies in Afro-Eurasia turned from an emphasis on largely separate developments with connections to other regions to an increasing focus on the benefits of connections, the possibilities of imitation, and the possibilities of diffusion.

   B. There is a fairly straight line from the interregional connections that developed in the postclassical period to what we now view as globalization.

      1. Of course, contemporary globalization involves far more rapid interactions and a greater volume of trade connections and far more extensive cultural interactions.

      2. Still, people who traded, traveled, and wrote travel accounts in the postclassical period inspired others who would extend interregional trading activities still further.

      3. Some historians argue that an evolutionary approach to the issue of globalization is misguided. Globalization, in their eyes, is a much newer phenomenon.

      4. Nonetheless, the postclassical explosion of trade and travel looms large in world history.

Further Reading:

Janet Abu-Lughod, *Before European Hegemony: The World System, A.D. 1250–1350.*

Milo Kearney, *The Indian Ocean in World History.*

Tansen Sen, *Buddhism, Diplomacy and Trade: The Realignment of Sino-Indian Relations, 600–1400.*

Questions to Consider:

1. During centuries when many people devoted themselves to one or another of the otherworldly religions, how could the interest in trade spread so widely? How can these two postclassical themes be reconciled?

2. What are the main advantages and drawbacks in thinking about this period as the dawn of a globalization process that continues to the present day?

Lecture Thirteen—Transcript
Postclassical Trade and Contacts

Our discussion today focuses on the development of new kinds of contacts, particularly trade contacts, in the postclassical period. In introducing the postclassical period, I've already argued that the new range and intensity of contacts was, along with the spread of world religions, one of the really crucial developments in this period, affecting most parts of Asia, many parts of Africa, and many parts of Europe. There was no single heroic event in this proliferation of contacts. We're talking really about the efforts of literally hundreds and thousands of traders, some inventors, some craftsmen, and certainly a lot of manufacturers, but the process can seem a little abstract. What I'd like to do in illustrating this crucial development is, first, talk about one of the interesting byproducts of the new patterns of contact in the emergence of a new set of world travelers. That will allow some personal faces on the phenomenon. Then, we'll turn back to the major routes themselves—and this is the most important part—talk about: "So what? What were the consequences of this contact? Why make such a big fuss about it?"

In the 14th century, one of the greatest—perhaps, *the* greatest—single world traveler emerged by the name of Ibn Battuta. Battuta was born in Morocco in northwestern Africa. He grew up in what we might call a middle-class merchant family, reasonably prosperous, and received a legal education. He launched his travels, as did so many Muslims, first by participating in the great, highly recommended, obligatory if possible, pilgrimage to Mecca. Battuta obviously crossed North Africa going to Mecca, and he already showed his travel thirst by not just visiting Mecca but by visiting other parts of the eastern Mediterranean—Palestine, Jordan, etc.

In his lifetime, Battuta would travel over 75,000 miles. Almost certainly, it was the longest set of trips any single individual had ever undertaken in world history. That's a lot of miles. He went by foot; he went on donkey—and the importance of donkeys in carrying world contacts at this point cannot be underestimated—he went occasionally on ship. He used virtually every known means of conveyance, but he undoubtedly spent a great a deal of time in motion. His travels would take him not just frequently back to the pilgrimage, to other parts of North Africa, and the Middle East, they took him to Persia. They took him well into Central Asia, where he frequently traveled over mountain passes in winter, enduring a number of harrowing adventures in the process. He spent a good bit of time in India, particularly in the Delhi sultanate, where he actually at one point had an official position. He traveled to island groups in the Indian Ocean. He traveled to Southeast Asia. He traveled to China—which as we will discuss further in a moment, he didn't actually like too well. After a long series of journeys, he then went back to North Africa but was still insatiable. In what we could regard as central or even slightly later middle age, he undertook a final set of trips into sub-Saharan Africa, particularly into the great kingdom of Mali.

He wrote up his travels, which is obviously why we know so much about them. His account both reflects the new range of geographical contact possible and also encouraged this kind of contact. Because people read Battuta, they could seek to imitate him. They could develop a thirst for learning about new places from his accounts. His motivations for travel seem to have been several. He was certainly religiously inspired. He was a faithful Muslim, and much of his travel—indeed, most of it—centered on territories that were fully or partly converted to Islam, where he could feel comfortable and maintain contact with his religious rituals.

His travel was sometimes probably sexually motivated. He writes rather self-satisfiedly about some sexual exploits during his travels. He frequently picked up consorts and short-lived spousal relationships. Sometimes, he probably left because these relationships deteriorated. Above all, he was clearly driven by a massive curiosity about strange places—even though often Muslim, still nevertheless strange.

In addition to illustrating the new potential for geographical expression of human curiosity, his accounts reflect a couple of other features that are worth noting. He judged according to the standards of Islam. In places that were Muslim but not exactly like the Middle East and North Africa, he would praise their religious piety—this particularly applies to his reactions to some of the African societies he visited—he would praise their piety but deplore departures from the norm. For example, he worried greatly that many African women seemed to wear fewer clothes than they should by Middle Eastern standards and seemed to have a social presence, a confidence in public assertions in social settings that he found disturbing. In his one clear venture well outside Islam, his visit to China, he professed himself—and it's a really interesting passage—almost clearly uncomfortable. He knew that China was a great society. He praised Chinese cities, architecture, etc., but he said he stuck to his room a lot because without the presence of an Islamic overlay, this was just a little bit disorienting.

Another great traveler of the postclassical period—actually, a little earlier than Ibn Battuta—was, of course, Marco Polo, the great Venetian traveler who presumably went to China under Mongol rule and reported elaborately on what he found there. A brief caveat: We are not absolutely sure that Marco Polo went. His uncles clearly visited China, but he may have used their accounts plus Persian travel literature to fabricate a version of his own travels, among other things, glorifying his personal exploits. We're simply not absolutely sure. The odd thing is that he fails to mention certain features of China that you think he would have found really quite noteworthy— for example, the foot binding of many Chinese women in the cities. So we're not absolutely sure, but if Marco Polo didn't do it, other Europeans clearly did. Their travels were somewhat less wide-ranging than Ibn Battuta's, though the travelers to China sometimes came back via the Indian Ocean; therefore, they encountered South and Southeast Asia, as well as East Asia. But the European travelers, if Marco Polo is taken as illustrative, differed from Ibn Battuta in one respect. They were less uncomfortable in settings outside their religious orbit. They almost had to be less uncomfortable because Christianity had spread less widely. They could not have expected a cultural umbrella that would frame them as a Muslim could expect.

But, if you put the two cases together—Ibn Battuta, Marco Polo or the Polos [his uncles]—you have an active sense of the new extent to which people could visit distance places, did visit distance places, and developed a thirst for travel adventure. In their ensuing accounts—Marco Polo's book, for example, was on Christopher Columbus's bookshelf somewhat later on—they spurred other people to seek trade activities and contact activities that would push them also into the unknown or at least the less known.

Travel, of course, was interesting. It's very clear that travel in this period differed greatly from the kinds of travel that had been possible in the earlier classical era. The travelers traveled farther, they encountered far more different kinds of situations, and their accounts are much more consistently accurate than accounts of earlier travelers, such as Herodotus, who simply made things up or accepted fabulous stories when he went beyond his actual travel range. This is a different kind of travel; it reflects a different kind of world.

The actual contact patterns need to be further embellished, as well. As I noted earlier, the core route for this new pattern of contact that emerged in the postclassical period was an Indian Ocean route connecting western Asia or the Middle East—the Arab territories, the Persian territories under Islam now—with South Asia, Southeast Asia, and the Pacific coast of China. This was a series of routes, initially forged by Arab merchants primarily, but soon joined by Muslims and others from India, Southeast Asia, and elsewhere and also a number of Persians. This was a series of routes that carried a variety of goods. Particularly important were manufactured goods from China, silk of course, but now also porcelain and some other products, and spices that were available from Southeast Asia or India.

This was an Asian-centered trade pattern, and it had the interesting effect—and here we begin to see the new importance of these kinds of contacts—of spurring major manufacturing expansions, particularly in China. In China, during the Song dynasty, which opened up in the late 10th century, some historians have actually referred to a Chinese industrial revolution. I think the term's a little misleading. We don't want to confuse it with industrialization later on, but there's no question that China was becoming, in this period, something of a world manufacturing powerhouse, a status that the nation seems to be recovering in our own day.

Other routes, of course, fed into the east-west contact. Three patterns were particularly important. As we've noted previously, two routes connected sub-Saharan Africa to this east-west trade and carried African goods not just into the Middle East and North Africa but into other parts of Asia, as well. The easiest route, the one that most clearly linked with the east-west corridor, was the coastal route that stretched up the Swahili coastline, along the Swahili trading cities that developed on the coast and on the islands of East Africa. But West African trading activities, merchants from places such as Ghana and Mali, also participated actively in interregional trade, using camels and horses to cross the Sahara, and seeing North

African traders come down to participate directly, as well, as traders and, once in a while, as raiders. Link number one was the connections that linked various parts of sub-Saharan Africa to the North African-Middle Eastern end of the east-west route. From Africa came a variety of goods—gold, slaves, exotic animals, certain other kinds of animal and vegetable products—that fed a considerable trade, particularly with the Middle East but also sometimes beyond. Handfuls of African slaves even showed up in postclassical China, where one can speculate about what the Chinese made of these peoples and, above all, what these people themselves made of their experience in such a different kind of environment.

Another feeder route developed beginning in the 8th and 9th centuries from Scandinavia through what is presently western Russia and Ukraine, passing through the great city of Kiev on its way to the Byzantine Empire and, from there, connecting with Arab trade, as well. Scandinavian traders coming down through Russia may actually have given Russia its name, from the Scandinavian word for "red," the red hair that many of these traders had. We don't know that for sure, but it's at least possible. Bu, there's no question that this East-Central European north-south route was a vital one for the region itself, as it contributed products and merchant activity to the larger east-west flow.

Slightly later and more gradually, Western Europe also connected with this trade route, as merchants from England, the Low Countries, and France began to come down, either overland or along the Atlantic coast to the Mediterranean, where they could directly reach into Middle Eastern areas in the eastern Mediterranean—Egypt, etc.

An example of this kind of merchant activity was the famous French merchant of the 15th century Jacques Coeur, who was an advisor to French kings, a money lender, but also who frequently traveled to the Middle East in search of products that would sell widely back home. He was just one of many European traders—French, obviously; Italian; and many others—who made considerable fortunes—and sometimes lost them, as well—in their connections with this new level of international commercial activity. Jacques Coeur ironically [was] disgraced in his later life [and] died on a crusade directed presumably against Islam and in favor of Christian reconquest of the Holy Land. A major set of routes then stretched from the Middle Eastern center to various parts of Asia. It was connected to much of Africa and a good bit of Europe, both east-central and west. The combination provided a series of activities that really had no previous precedent in world history.

What were the results? Why make such a fuss about this? A number of results developed from these trading patterns that were important at the time and that also set precedents for later activity. I mentioned one already. The extent to which this level of interregional trade could now have a major impact on internal economies, particularly the economy of China, was already an effect of no small magnitude. Some areas of the world—again, particularly in China—began to orient a good bit of their economic activity toward production for what we today call world markets. New kinds of consumer dependence developed, as well. We don't usually think of postclassical societies as consumer societies and, in a modern sense, they weren't. But very clearly in this period—and there had been hints of it earlier along the Silk Roads—certain elements of the upper classes in a number of societies developed tastes for goods that could be only supplied from distant regions. A clear example occurred in Western Europe during and after the Crusades. The Crusades began in the later 11th century. As West Europeans, particularly noblemen, participated in the Crusades, they learned of higher living standards that were common in Middle Eastern cities, and they developed a taste for some of the resultant products. A particularly interesting example that would motivate a tremendous amount of European activity from this point onward into the 19th century, a case in point, is sugar. Postclassical Europeans traditionally had sweetened their products with honey, which actually strikes me as quite sensible and quite pleasant. But for whatever reason—and I cannot pretend to know why—they liked sugar better. They couldn't make it at home, so they began an obvious and consistent effort to acquire access to more regular supplies of sugar—initially, still for the upper classes; this is not yet a mass taste, although it will become one. This kind of consumer attachment obviously helped feed the activities of many merchants, both European and Asian. It helped spur new kinds of shipping activities in the Mediterranean that would link Europe to Middle Eastern ports where products could be transshipped from other parts of Asia. This kind of a consumer attachment was itself a major variable in world history from this point onward.

Not all societies developed equal levels of susceptibility to consumer needs. China, for example, which had an elaborate urban consumer culture in the postclassical period, needed far fewer products from the outside world than did Western Europe. China did need to trade with Southeast Asia, particularly for certain kinds of tea, but their needs were otherwise limited. China would see a much greater effort to seek from world trade other kinds of products than personal consumer items—products such as exotic animals for zoos; handfuls, not masses, but handfuls of slaves; and particularly, precious metals. As these goods moved along the new trade routes in response to the supply of Chinese manufactured products, there were new kinds of economic impact, consumer attachments, and even dependence on international trade.

A third item, obviously, was a new level of cultural contact. Some of this involves simply a matter of word exchange from one language to the next. A large number of words began to pass into European languages from Arabic, denoting the kinds of products that were now being transshipped from other parts of the world to Europe. Terms such as *orange*, for example, or *sugar* are Arabic words translated into the major European languages because these were the words that described, initially, what the products themselves were. But other kinds of cultural exchange were obviously even more important. Particularly noteworthy was the extent to which what Europeans called the Arabic numbering system came into wide use in this period. This system had been developed in classical India. It was not Arabic, but the Arabs had taken it over from the Indians. Europeans and others would, in this period, take it over from the Arabs, providing what is still the most efficient numbering system ever developed in the world, a numbering system that now began to gain what we would today call some real international currency.

Mathematical systems could spread more widely. *Algebra*, another Arabic word and Arabic mathematical innovation, began to spread from the Arab world to other societies, including Europe. Not surprisingly, then, new levels of commercial contact spurred other kinds of cultural interaction even across what otherwise seemed major religious barriers—for example, the barrier between Islam and Christianity.

Technologies were impacted by new levels of world trade in two ways. First, a number of new technologies were introduced during the postclassical period deliberately to facilitate new kinds of trading activities, particularly new kinds of seagoing commercial activities.

Ship design improved. The Arabs introduced significant developments in sailing ships, particularly making them more appropriate for use in the Indian Ocean. Toward the end of the postclassical period, the Chinese introduced gigantic oceangoing vessels, the Chinese junks with huge hulls and huge carrying capacity that they began to use from the Song dynasty onward to link eastern China with the Indian Ocean trade routes.

In addition to new ship design, new navigational devices emerged. The compass was almost certainly invented in China, possibly, initially, not for use by travelers, but to help the Chinese arrange their domestic furnishings appropriately, according to the principles of *feng shui*. Whether this story is entirely accurate or not, the navigational use of the compass was quickly realized, and the Chinese used the compass increasingly in their own commercial activities. From the Chinese, the compass would spread to Southeast Asia, to the Middle East, and to Europe, where in a number of its transmissions, the device was also improved, particularly for shipboard use. Other navigational devices in the period included the astrolabe, which helped ships locate themselves according to the night sky. A number of devices facilitated navigation, and obviously, this is both a consequence of heightened levels of interregional trade and, again, an encouragement to further levels of trade.

The second technological impact of this new level of contact involves transmission. Not surprisingly, although still slowly by contemporary standards, new levels of contact help societies learn about inventions that had initially been introduced elsewhere more quickly than had previously been the case. Technological diffusion was not new; agriculture, iron use, etc., had previously spread from one area to another, but now the process is accelerated and, in some cases, made much more deliberate than had been the case earlier. An interesting example, which also I admit shows the continuing limitations on the process, was paper.

Paper was a product that had been invented in classical China and not used widely outside of China at that point. The utility of paper in China, a society that was particularly bureaucratic, can't escape notice, but the fact is that this was a major technological invention that could greatly facilitate communication. Arabs learned about paper in their military interactions in western China in the 8th and 9th centuries. They captured a number of Chinese and took them back to the Middle East. They discovered that a couple of them knew how to make paper, and they put them to work setting up the first paper-manufacturing operation in the Middle East proper, as I say, in the 8th and 9th centuries. Western Europeans would learn about paper from their contact with the Arabs, and the first European paper factory was established in Sicily, reasonably close to the Middle East, in the very early 1200s. Now, again, this is not lightening transmission. You're talking about several centuries between Arab utilization of paper and West European imitation from the Arabs. Nevertheless, this is a lot faster than we've seen major technologies transmitted heretofore, and we will have other examples in subsequent sessions of technological transmissions during the postclassical period that were more rapid still.

Economic impact, consumer tastes, cultural exchanges, technological diffusion—all of these added up to a significant set of consequences of environmental factors surrounding the new level of interregional contacts.

The final point in talking about consequence really sums up the growing utility that various societies in Asia, Africa, and Europe found in maintaining or increasing their commitment to these international activities. The fact was that the utility of international activities or interregional connections was so obvious at this point that some kind of interregional system would survive disruptions or changes in the original system itself. Most obviously, as we noted in a previous discussion, the Arab capacity to sustain major initiatives in the interregional arena began to decline in the 12th and 13th centuries. Arabs remained involved; other Muslims from the Middle East and South Asia continued to participate strongly, but the international apparatus could have tumbled, at least for a while, as Arab capacity diminished and as Arab political and cultural vitality dwindled to some extent. But the system was simply too precious to abandon. As the Arabs' sustaining of the system yielded to other entrants, the clear result was a continued commitment, a continued capacity to sustain interregional contacts, either along the established trade routes or on alternative routes that would develop precisely because of this new level of commitment, this new understanding of resulting benefits.

The postclassical period—particularly, as interregional connections developed and solidified by 1000 CE onward—this has been seen, as we discussed previously, as one of the real watersheds in world history. [This was] the point at which many societies in Afro-Eurasia turned from an emphasis on largely separate developments with connections with other regions—a peripheral activity at best—turned from this focus on the local and regional to an increasing focus on the benefits of connections, the possibilities of imitation, and the possibilities of diffusion. This was a pattern that would, then, once the tipping point occurred, continue to accelerate from this juncture onward.

There's another way to make the same point. I do this tentatively, but it's worth consideration. There is a fairly straight line from the interregional connections that developed in the postclassical period to what we now view as globalization. Now, there are lots of apologies. Contemporary globalization is a lot quicker. It involves a lot greater volume in terms of trade connections and far more extensive cultural interactions, so the postclassical period does not introduce globalization in the contemporary sense, but the straight-line aspect is nevertheless noteworthy. People who traded, traveled, and wrote about their activities in the postclassical period helped inspire people who would extend interregional trading activities still further later on, people such as Christopher Columbus. They, in turn, would feed great trading companies, new technologies that would spur travel and trade still further in the 19th century and on to contemporary globalization. There are historians—and we'll encounter them later in the course—who will argue that this evolutionary approach, a pattern of interregional connections from the postclassical period blossoming steadily and gradually into globalization, is the wrong view. Globalization, in their eyes, is a much newer phenomenon, and we will have to deal with that. But remember this possibility. This is why the postclassical explosion of trade and travel really looms so large in world history. It's a different world by the 11th and 12th centuries in terms of the impact and involvement of many people—merchants, consumers, upper-class leaders—the involvement of many people in a dependence on and enjoyment of contacts with distance places.

Lecture Fourteen
Postclassical Patterns of Imitation

Scope:

Many societies in which the apparatus of civilization was fairly new used the opportunity provided by contacts with neighboring older societies to copy aspects of culture, technology, and social structure. This is a further illustration of the importance of the new interregional network, though the imitations were on a regional rather than a global level. Japan, Russia, and Western Europe provide examples of the process, which includes other cases, such as Vietnam and Korea in East Asia and the Southeast Asian importation of religious and artistic forms from India, China, and later the Middle East. Imitation helps provide some common themes and comparative opportunities for the otherwise diffuse process of civilization expansion. It also raises questions, however, about civilization definition: Was Japan part of a larger, Chinese-dominated East Asian civilization, or did it remain so different from China that it should be handled separately? How is Russia to be treated in relation to other parts of Christian Europe? Finally, the process of imitation did not extend well to politics, where attempts to copy larger government models largely failed in favor of more decentralized systems. Here, too, is a common dynamic among the imitative societies, though a somewhat negative one.

Outline

I. In this lecture, we will look at patterns of imitation in Japan, Russia, Southeast Asia, and briefly, Western Europe during the postclassical period. In the process, we will touch on a number of key themes.

   A. First, we will continue with the theme of interregional contacts, but in these cases, the distances are smaller than those we saw in the last lecture.

   B. We will also see the continuing spread of civilization.

   C. Finally, we will see that these regions were different in terms of cultural systems, religions, political systems, and trade patterns, but we will also note a common process of increasing convergence in which societies deliberately undertook activities that would bring them closer to adjacent, more prosperous societies without fully merging with them.

II. Early in the postclassical period and continuing for at least a century, Japan organized expeditions to China in search of trade and knowledge. The Japanese came to imitate China in an impressive range of sectors.

   A. The Japanese learned new agricultural and manufacturing techniques from the Chinese that spurred development of the Japanese economy.

   B. Japan also took up much of the culture and cultural apparatus of China, including its writing system, basic verse styles, martial arts, the art of gardening, and Buddhism; with Buddhism came architectural forms such as the pagoda and temple.

   C. Chinese social ideas were adopted in Japan to a limited extent.

      1. The prestige of merchants declined slightly in Japan.

      2. The Japanese did not import the full range of Chinese thought about gender relations, but they did learn from the Chinese that women were less equal to men than the Japanese had previously believed.

   D. Japan adopted something of China's superior attitude toward the wider world.

   E. One reason that the Japanese did not attempt a larger expansion effort in this period may be that their horizons were limited by the idea that they had nothing to learn from places other than China.

III. Trade ran through western Russia and the Ukraine during the postclassical period, connecting Russia with the Byzantine Empire.

   A. Russians traveled to Constantinople for political missions and cultural exchange, and Byzantine emissaries were active in Russia.

   B. The Russians got their writing system and religion from the Byzantine Empire.

C. Along with religion and writing came a larger cultural apparatus conditioned by the extent to which Russia was a less prosperous, less sophisticated society than Byzantium. Byzantine architectural styles were imitated, along with the Byzantine tradition of iconography.

D. From the Byzantines, Russian leaders incorporated at least some sense of political horizons. A kind of historical chain was believed to link Rome to Byzantium to Russia.

IV. Japan and Russia exhibited similarities in the basic process of adoption and adaptation.

A. In each instance, people in the imitating society believed that there was a positive advantage in visiting and copying aspects of the adjacent, more prosperous society.

B. This process raises a question that is crucial for the postclassical period: now that civilization is expanding and societies are deliberately imitating each other, how do we define a civilization?

1. In the Japanese case, Japan imitated China, but it did not become Chinese.

2. The efficiency of identifying an East Asian civilization zone probably outweighs the drawbacks, but the label is clearly an oversimplification.

3. We can view Russia as a partial heir to a Byzantine/East European tradition that distinguishes it from Western Europe; thus, we have two major civilization zones in Europe: the West and the East-Central East.

V. In the postclassical period, a number of regional kingdoms emerged in Southeast Asia. At the same time, this region received significant cultural and commercial influence from other sources, notably, India.

A. Indian traders sometimes brought Hinduism into this region, and the spread of Buddhism from India was even more striking. From India also came inspiration for regional writing systems.

B. Chinese influence is seen here, particularly in the form of increasing trade activity from the time of the Song dynasty onward.

C. By the end of the postclassical period, Islam had gained the greatest religious success in many parts of this region.

D. This pattern of varying outside influences combined with local traditions sets up a different model in Southeast Asia from that seen in Japan and Russia.

VI. Western Europe did not have the same needs that Japan and Russia did from its influences, but West European leaders saw clear advantages in imitating certain aspects of the Byzantine Empire and the Arab world.

A. Western Europe used these contacts to regain knowledge of classical learning that had been preserved by the Byzantines and Arabs.

B. From the Muslims and the Byzantines, Western Europeans also copied a variety of technologies and benefited from Arab advances in medicine, mathematics, and other fields.

C. The Arab philosophical debate over the boundaries between faith and reason was transmitted to Europe, where it was applied to Christian interests in rationalism.

D. The Gothic arch—that quintessential artistic symbol of postclassical Western Europe—was, in part, adapted from the characteristic Islamic arch.

E. Western Europe borrowed from Islamic innovations in commercial law, identifying principles that could transcend political boundaries and protect merchants regardless of specific location.

F. Whether acknowledged or not, the Western European debt to Islamic and Byzantine examples was considerable. The fact that this period was one of extensive imitation is an important addition to our understanding of postclassical Western Europe.

VII. The imitation process raises one final question for the period itself and carries some interesting implications for more contemporary situations.

A. In all four cases, cultural forms and styles, along with technologies, seem to have been particularly eagerly sought. Why is this so?

B. One fact that prompts this question is the lack of success with the imitation of political forms.

    1. Japan, Russia, and Western Europe were aware that political models existed that were superior to their own decentralized situations. As Japan began to imitate China, for example, it exhibited a deliberate desire to import the Chinese imperial system.

    2. For almost a century, the Chinese example was incorporated into Japanese political activity, but the effort failed because Japan could not sustain the same degree of centralization as China.

    3. The Japanese solution, during the bulk of the postclassical period, would be a form of feudalism.

C. Russian leaders were aware of Byzantine political examples, but they did not wield the same power and could not establish a tightly organized political system.

D. The Western Europeans had a chance to establish a more centralized political structure under Charlemagne in the early 9th century.

    1. Charlemagne's realm extended to northern Italy, very northern Spain, France, the Low Countries, and parts of western Germany.

    2. Charlemagne, however, lacked the resources and, possibly, the experience to set up an independent bureaucracy.

    3. Charlemagne ended up reinforcing Western European feudalism.

E. We see here societies that are capable of imitating models to speed up artistic, literary, and cultural development, but are the imitators inherently less able to use political examples?

    1. Is a period of cultural gestation necessary before a society can imitate another society's political achievements, and if so, does this characteristic still apply in the world today?

    2. We have a number of instances today in which societies seek or are told to seek political inspiration from countries that have different political experience. Are such models particularly difficult to follow, or is the political delay we have noted confined to the postclassical period?

VIII. The postclassical period saw a great deal of deliberate imitation and a substantial degree of success in this arena.

    A. Connections were forged between societies that were new to the civilization phenomenon and those in which civilization patterns were better established, but these connections never completely erased issues of definition between such civilizations as Russia and Byzantium or Japan and China.

    B. In three of the major cases—Japan, Russia, and Western Europe—the societies involved were on the peripheries of the most sophisticated patterns available during the postclassical period. These three societies would use this period of imitation as gestation for a later, stronger, emergence in world history.

Further Reading:

Charles Freeman, *The Closing of the Western Mind: The Rise of Faith and the Fall of Reason.*

David R. Knechtges and Eugene Vance, eds., *Rhetoric and the Discourses of Power in Court Culture: China, Europe, and Japan.*

Nicholas Riasanovsky and Mark Steinberg, *A History of Russia*, 7th ed.

Questions to Consider:

1. Why was so much attention devoted to imitating cultural building blocks and artistic and intellectual forms? How does this compare to processes of imitation today?

2. How did Western Europe's imitation process differ from that of Japan or Russia? Were the differences significant?

Lecture Fourteen—Transcript
Postclassical Patterns of Imitation

We're talking in this session—briefly, I admit—about four different parts of the world during the postclassical period. We'll talk about Japan, Russia, Southeast Asia, and briefly, Western Europe. The main focus is on patterns of imitation that these four areas conducted—usually fairly deliberately—with adjacent regions that were, in some measurable senses, better developed. They had older cultures; they had greater cities; they had greater prosperity; and they had a more elaborate apparatus with regard to technology. We're touching base here with a number of key themes. Obviously, we continue the notion of interregional contacts, but now we're talking about slightly smaller distances than the ones we were referring to in the great systems we discussed in the previous lecture.

We're talking certainly about the spread of civilization. The parts of the world we're talking about today either had been outside the civilization orbit in the classical period or at least only incompletely involved. We're very definitely talking about an effort to make this expansion of civilization manageable and meaningful in a world history sense. We're talking, without question, about four places that were very different. Western Europe was different from Russia; Russia, obviously, [was] different from Southeast Asia—differences that would show up in cultural systems, in religions, in at least the details of political systems, in specific trade patterns, all those things. We're not talking about a nice, coherent package, but we are talking about something of a common process—and it's really an intriguing one—in which societies deliberately undertook activities that would bring them closer with adjacent, more prosperous societies without fully merging with them, but in a process that gives specific meaning to the notion of increasing convergence that we've introduced in previous discussions.

The first case—and, in some senses, it's the easiest one because the process was so very explicit—is that of Japan. Quite early in the postclassical period, Japanese leaders—princes—began to send student trips to China in order to learn more about Chinese ways and to bring their knowledge back to Japan proper. This began a century's long flirtation between Japan and China, in which Japan would regularly organize expeditions several times a year to reach

China in search of trade but also in search of knowledge. In the process, the Japanese developed a really impressive range of sectors in which they imitated China substantially or, at least, in part. Obviously, there was technological imitation. The Japanese were able to learn new agricultural techniques from the Chinese, new manufacturing techniques that began to spur the increasing development of the Japanese economy. We don't necessarily want to argue that Japan became as sophisticated technologically as China was, but there was certainly interchange. This was a pretty obvious aspect of the regular kinds of connections that developed between the two societies.

The second area—and, in some ways, the more elaborate still in which imitation had massive effects—was in the area of culture and cultural apparatus. In the first place, quite simply, the Japanese introduced the Chinese writing system. This was a system designed for a very different language. Japanese and Chinese remain very different as spoken languages. Over time, the Chinese ideographic system proved not fully appropriate for Japanese and some other systems were developed, but they all built from this system and the Chinese system was retained, as well. Simply put—though ultimately with some modifications—the Japanese got writing, one of the basic components of civilization, from the Chinese. They also incorporated a number of other cultural forms, adapting them, of course, to Japanese language and other conditions. They introduced many of the basic Chinese verse styles; they adapted Chinese martial arts; they adapted Chinese systems of very carefully regulated gardens; they adopted Buddhism extensively from China—ironically, adopting it more wholeheartedly than the Chinese would during the postclassical period as a whole. With Buddhism from China also came architectural forms, such as the pagoda, the temple form, and a variety of other artistic themes that would connect Japanese art with Chinese. Cultural connections, then, were extremely substantial and helped shape a real blossoming of Japanese culture in a number of artistic areas.

Chinese social ideas were adapted to a somewhat more limited extent. Among other things, for example, as Japan learned from China, the prestige of merchants began to decline slightly, although the Chinese downgrading of merchants in the Confucian system was never fully brought into Japan. Another interesting area involved gender relations. The Japanese did not import the full gamut of

Chinese gender relations; most notably, they did not import foot binding. But from the Chinese, they did learn that women were less equal to men than the Japanese had previously thought; gender divisions tended to increase in Japan, though without reaching Chinese levels. There was an interesting footnote to this at some points in the postclassical period: Because Chinese culture was such an object of esteem, it was assumed that Japanese men should emphasize Chinese culture, which left Japanese writing actually to women for an interesting period of time. Among other things, the first novel ever written in the world, *The Tale of Genji*, was written by a Japanese woman in this period, where it was all right for women to do this because the real prestige stuff was stuff being done in the Chinese manner by men. Social limitation, then, was significant but obviously less complete than the kinds of connections that developed in culture and technology.

A final area—and an intriguing one—where the Japanese seemed to have learned from the Chinese involved attitudes toward the wider world. China, as is well known, tended to think of itself as the epitome of civilization, with all other societies viewed as inferior and barbarian. The Japanese picked up something of this attitude by osmosis, obviously arguing that Japan, in connection with China, was a very special place and little attention needed to be paid to the rest of the world. One world historian has actually wondered why Japan, in this period of clearly increased dynamism, didn't attempt a larger expansion effort, for example, possibly sailing into the Pacific. We obviously don't know the answer. It's hard to answer historical negatives, but one reason may be that the Japanese were so focused on China and, through this, [had] a sense that there was nothing to learn from other places, that the horizons were interestingly shaped and, possibly, interestingly limited.

The second imitation example involves Russia and the Byzantine Empire. We've seen already how trade ran through western Russia and the Ukraine, what's technically known as Kievan Rus during this period, and connected it to the Byzantine Empire. With trade obviously came other kinds of missions. Russians frequently went to Constantinople for trading purposes, political missions, and cultural exchange—that sort of thing. Byzantine emissaries were active in Russia, as well, [with] missionary activity at the forefront. From these connections, Russia imported a variety of things from the

Byzantine Empire. Cultural apparatus, again, was primary. The Russians got their writing system from the Byzantine Empire, from the Cyrillic adaptation of the Greek alphabet that was exported widely to east-central Europe, including Russia. Along with writing, the Russians, of course, got religion. The decision to emphasize Orthodox Christianity presumably involved this effort by Vladimir, the ruler of Russia, to distinguish among three options: Islam was rejected because it didn't allow alcohol; Western Catholicism was rejected because the Russians were worried about too much papal interference. That left the Orthodox faith, but frankly, there probably wasn't all that much choice given the Russian connections with Byzantium. This must have seemed quite obvious.

Along with religion and writing came a wider cultural apparatus conditioned only by the extent to which Russia was a less prosperous, less sophisticated urban society than Byzantium. But Byzantine architectural styles were widely imitated. Particularly interesting was the Russian adoption of the Byzantine tradition of iconography, of carefully worked paintings of saints, at which the Russians would ultimately become past masters, but which they did not, in fact, originate. Artistic, religious cultures were widely imported, along with the basic apparatus of cultural transmission itself, the writing system. From the Byzantines, also, Russian leaders incorporated at least some sense of political horizons. To the Russians, the Byzantine Empire was the successor to Rome, and there could seem to be some sort of chain that connected Rome to Byzantium to Russia. We will see this notion blossom in the next period of world history still more fully. Cultural imitation was primary. Some technologies no doubt [were transmitted], but a political orientation was transmitted, as well.

Japan and Russia, two very different places imitating two very different societies—simply using China or the Byzantine Empire as models ensures differentiation—nevertheless, [the two] exhibit some striking similarities in terms of basic process. In each instance, various people in the imitating society feel that there's positive advantage not only in visiting but also in copying aspects of the adjacent, more prosperous society. Cultural imitation seems to play a strikingly significant role, although other kinds of apparatus and ideas could be imported, as well. The process raises one other question that actually is crucial for the postclassical period and, to some extent, new in this period. It's a question that we will have to deal with at various points from this juncture onward. The question is: How, now that civilization is expanding and societies are deliberately imitating each other, do you define civilization? The Japanese case is probably particularly clear. Japan imitated China. It did not, however, become Chinese. It didn't or couldn't imitate fully. Now that civilization has reached Japan as a form of human organization, do we need to talk about Japanese civilization, as well as Chinese? Or can we talk about a larger East Asian civilization zone, in which Chinese influences are primary, but in which other societies, not only Japan but also Korea and Vietnam, sort of hover, participating in a number of common influences—including various aspects of cultural styles, including some exposure to Buddhism, certainly some exposure to Confucianism—but without becoming a clearly unified whole? It's a choice. You can answer either way. The advantage of seeing Japan as a separate civilization is that you have to make fewer apologies. You have to back up less frequently and say, but don't forget, Japan and China differed on this point. On the other hand, there's an obvious inefficiency. If we start labeling Japan a separate civilization, what do you do then with Korea and Vietnam? How many civilizations do you end up with, and can you manage them? The efficiency of an East Asian civilization zone probably outweighs its drawbacks, but it clearly has drawbacks. It oversimplifies—[it's] a choice.

The case of Russia is actually also intriguing, and we will have to encounter it later, as well. World historians, frankly, have a good bit of trouble dealing with Russia. They don't quite know whether to say it's part of European civilization because, after all, it becomes Christian, or it is part of a special Byzantine tradition, but it's not fully Byzantine. What do you do with it? My personal preference is to view Russia as a partial heir to a Byzantine-East European tradition that will continue to distinguish it from Western Europe; thus, [we have] two major civilization zones emerging in Europe, the West and the East-Central East. But this is disputable and, among other things, it raises the question of where you draw the boundary line in East-Central Europe. Among other things, it seems to fluctuate fairly often. There's no fully happy resolution to this dilemma, but the main point is to recognize it's a dilemma. Because imitation is becoming more important, the clear-cut boundary lines that separate one cultural zone from another are blurring. We simply have to recognize that fact and recognize that some new kinds of choices, some new kinds of dilemmas, emerge in consequence.

The case of Southeast Asia is somewhat different. This was a period, the postclassical, in which a number of regional kingdoms emerged in Southeast Asia—in Thailand, in Burma, in parts of present-day Malaysia, and in parts of Indonesia. At the same time, this was a region that received significant cultural and commercial influence from several other sources. Most important, initially, was, of course, India. We've noted earlier that Indian traders reached into this region and sometimes brought with them Hinduism. The spread of Buddhism from India was even more striking. From India, also, came inspiration for a number of regional writing systems, which were adapted but, nevertheless, which utilized the Indian model. An Indian derivation remains extremely significant, but Chinese influence would come in, as well, particularly in the form of increasing trade activity from the Song dynasty onward. This, among other things, began to establish communities of Chinese merchants in certain parts of Southeast Asia. This would expand later on, as well. The Indian influence is modified by Chinese contacts. Then, by the end of the postclassical period, a third stream of influence is coming in, in the form of Islam and Islamic merchants, actually gaining the greatest religious success in many parts of this region of any of the three influences. Southeast Asia, then, is a region that clearly is an active recipient of outside influences, an active zone of commercial exchange and travel exchange, but in which the fact that several different influences combined with local traditions sets up a pattern that's rather different from the Japanese and Russian cases, where there's a single model that the societies attempted to follow.

Western Europe constitutes the fourth major case in the pattern we're discussing today. West Europe obviously needed some things less than Japan and Russia did from its potential inspirers. It already had an alphabet inherited from classical Rome. Through missionary activities early in the postclassical period, it already had a religion, although in one sense, this religion is borrowed. It's not native to Western Europe, as is well known. But West Europe did see the advantage. West European leaders of various sorts—political, cultural, and economic—did see clear advantages in imitating contacts, both with the Byzantine Empire and with the Arab world. In part, as is quite well known in medieval European history, it utilized these contacts to regain knowledge of classical learning—

scientific and philosophical, particularly, literary to some extent—because the Byzantines and the Arabs preserved Hellenistic and Roman knowledge better than had been the case in West Europe itself. But imitating the classics via these models is really not the main point. From the Muslims and from the Byzantines, West Europeans also imitated a variety of technologies, and the eagerness of West European technological imitation becomes a striking aspect of the postclassical period. It imitated scientific concepts. Again, partly these were derived from Greek and Hellenistic work, but Europeans also benefited very directly from Arab advances in medicine, in mathematics, and in other fields. The West Europeans borrowed philosophically. The Arab debate over the boundaries between faith and reason was a debate that was transmitted back into Europe, where it made a great deal of sense in terms of Christian interests in rationalism, as well. There was significant borrowing in the area of art. The Gothic arch—that quintessential artistic symbol of postclassical Western Europe—was in part adapted from the characteristic Islamic arch. The engineering principles were essentially the same and the stylistic features were very similar.

Legal imitations also occurred. West Europe borrowed extensively from Islamic innovations in commercial law—among other things, learning that one could identify certain principles of commercial law that could transcend political boundaries and help protect merchants, regardless of specific location. The West European debt, in other words—whether acknowledged or not—to Islamic and Byzantine examples was considerable. This is not a case exactly [the same] as that of Japan and Russia. The imitation is a little more diffuse. Two societies are being utilized, not just one. But the notion of this as an extensive period of Western imitation is an important addition—or at least a heightened emphasis—for our view of postclassical Western Europe in this larger world history period. We need to talk, as we will next time, about what this partial revision does to our sense of the emergence of Western civilization more generally.

The imitation process, going back to the general phenomenon, raises one final question that's actually intriguing for the period itself and possibly carries some interesting implications even for more contemporary situations. Particularly with Japan and Russia, but really for all four cases, we've stressed the extent to which, along with technologies, cultural forms and styles seem to have been particularly eagerly sought. One wonders why. Were these simply what were most impressive about the societies when student groups or merchants visited—the great buildings, the great artistic works, and the polished literature—or, as these new civilization regions were beginning to get going in the civilization process, was there a need first to establish some cultural bases before other things could be done? Because the striking omission from the pattern of imitation, though not for want of trying, was the significant capacity to imitate the model in the area of politics. Here, we need to go back to three separate stories—stories with ultimately the same point.

Japan, Russia, and Western Europe were keenly aware that political models existed that were considerably superior to their own decentralized political situations. As Japan began to imitate China, there was a deliberate and, frankly, quite understandable desire to import the Chinese imperial system. After all, Japanese princes were sponsoring the student voyages. They surely wished to enhance their own political power. What better way than to introduce a powerful notion of emperor, a powerful bureaucracy, supplemented by Confucianism? For the better part of the century, the Chinese example was widely incorporated into Japanese political activity. But the effort failed. Japan simply could not, at that point, sustain that degree of centralization. Mountain and island barriers possibly impeded; lack of political experience and legitimacy possibly impeded; but as Japan successfully imitated aspects of Chinese culture—economic activity, social forms—it notably departed from the Chinese example in politics. The Japanese solution during the bulk of the postclassical period would be a form of feudalism, a form of relationships between regional lords and vassals, that led to a great deal of internal warfare, could be utilized to construct some larger political patterns, and could be utilized to inspire larger systems of loyalty that many people have argued are extremely influential in Japanese history since that point, but which definitely did not generate anything like the Chinese political model.

With Russia, as we've already noted, Russian leaders were keenly aware of Byzantine political examples and Russian rulers were capable of pronouncements that could make them sound like junior-league Byzantine autocrats. They could say, "My subjects will do this; my subjects will convert to Christianity," as though they wielded the power of a great imperial bureaucracy. They did not. Russia had central rulers during much of the postclassical period—

some initially, perhaps, imported from Scandinavia—but they did not establish a tightly organized political system. There was a great deal of looseness, a great deal of negotiation and horse-trading between the ruler and local aristocrats. This was a decentralized political system, despite the existence of a clear centralized political model.

The West European case, broadly speaking, is just interestingly similar. The West Europeans had one clear shot at a more centralized, coordinated political structure, and this shot occurred under Charlemagne in the early 9th century. Charlemagne was clearly aware of the Roman Empire's example, but he was also aware of the Byzantine Empire and the Arab caliphate. There was a clear interest in developing a large central kingdom or empire, and Charlemagne's realm extended to northern Italy, very northern Spain, through France, the Low Countries, and parts of western Germany. It was an impressive geographic amalgam. Briefly, it looked as if Western Europe might beat the odds and, at an early phase of its development, manage to create a substantial and possibly sophisticated political structure, but as with the Japanese effort with China, this attempt failed. Charlemagne lacked the resources and, possibly, the experience to set up a really independent bureaucracy. He ended up reinforcing West European feudalism, which was a system interestingly similar to the Japanese fallback. Charlemagne's heirs, his grandsons, split his realm into three, hinting at the later development of France, on the one hand; Germany on the other; and then an intermediate territory that would always be something of a no man's land, embracing the Low Countries—Switzerland, northern Italy, etc. The effort simply foundered; West Europe during the postclassical period emerged as yet another society in which loose political structures and loose political rule predominated.

Here is the obvious question: Is this somehow a logical pattern, in which societies that prove quite capable of imitating aspects of other societies' cultures and who use the imitation rapidly to speed up artistic, literary, and cultural development, are these simply inherently less able to utilize political example? Does culture have to come first? Is there a period of political gestation necessary before a society can imitate another society's political achievements? If this is so, is this a case in point that still applies in the world today? We have a number of instances in the world today in which societies seek or are told to seek political inspiration from societies who have more political experience. Is this a particularly hard thing to imitate, or is the experience of the postclassical period, where politics clearly lagged behind culture, is this simply confined to that period and no longer applicable to the world today? I don't have an answer to this question, but I think the postclassical patterns do pose an intriguing question.

The postclassical period saw, obviously, a great deal of deliberate and substantial amount of successful imitation. New connections were forged between societies in which civilization was a new phenomenon and societies in which the patterns were better established. These connections were never complete. These connections never erased issues about civilization definition—as between Russia and Byzantium, Japan and China, etc.—but the fact that the questions could be raised at all suggests the importance of the imitation process.

One final point is equally obvious. At least three of the major cases explored today involve societies—Japan, Russia, and Western Europe—that during the postclassical period were clearly somewhat on the peripheries of the most sophisticated patterns available in the world at the time. They did not have as advanced economies. They did not generate the goods for trade that the more established centers did, and as we've just discussed, they clearly fell short of the political standards of China, the caliphate, or the Byzantine Empire. But these three societies—and, possibly, Southeast Asia should be tossed into the mix, as well—would use this period of imitation as gestation for a later emergence in world history in a much stronger fashion. Thus, we see this period not only as one of imitation but one of unwitting preparation of societies that would later play a much greater and more independent role on the world scene.

Lecture Fifteen
Western Civilization in World Context

Scope:

Western civilization is arguably a more elusive concept than Chinese, Indian, or Middle Eastern civilization. World history, including the comparative approach, raises interesting issues about identifying Western civilization. The postclassical period allows some of these issues to be sorted out, though the process must begin earlier. The tradition of teaching Western civilization reflected several factors: an imperialist-style belief that the West was possibly the only superior civilization; a concomitant concern, born in the ashes of World War I, that the West was falling apart and needed historical shoring up; and a belief on the American side that emphasis on Western values would help integrate a diverse and suspect pool of immigrants. Thus, Western civilization advocates tended to argue that there was a straight line from the earliest great civilizations to the glories of Western Europe later on. Beginning Western civilization with the river valleys, however, raises two questions: First, what was Western about them? And second, how can we account for the greater legacy of the river valleys to later East European and Middle Eastern societies? Should the Western tradition, then, be traced to the classical Mediterranean? This is certainly possible, though there is much about classical Greece and Rome that does not seem particularly Western; the societies themselves (particularly Greece) tended to look eastward. The first indisputably Western civilization, in fact, emerged in Western Europe during the postclassical period. It had several features that have survived, and it was, as we have seen, a somewhat underdeveloped borrower during the period. But by the later postclassical period, it was possible to identify a Western civilization and compare it with the Asian and African cases.

Outline

I. We will focus primarily on two questions with a bearing on the West as part of the postclassical world.
    A. First, when can an identifiable Western tradition be identified and what does that tradition consist of?

B. Second, how do we situate the West in the postclassical world?

    1. We have already begun this process by looking at Western Europe as one of several imitating societies with some distinctive twists.

    2. We will add some factors relating to particular patterns of Western trade and dynamism toward the end of the postclassical period.

C. It is impossible to teach a full Western civilization program in the framework of world history; thus we will look at a more subtle issue involving the Western civilization tradition, namely, the extent to which the West is sometimes viewed almost unanalytically.

II. We can begin by situating the West among certain other definitional issues previously evoked.

A. It is harder to pinpoint the origins and characteristics of Western tradition than of Chinese or Indian tradition.

B. One problem in looking at the classical Mediterranean tradition as the origin of the West is the extent to which this tradition fed not only the West but also a number of other societies, including Eastern Europe and the Arab world.

    1. This fact makes it difficult to extract exactly what is Western in this tradition.

    2. The same thing holds true in the great debate between rationalism and faith.

C. Another problem in overemphasizing the classical origins of a Western tradition involves how much of the classical tradition did not survive or, at least, did not survive in any direct sense.

    1. Classical Greek and Roman attitudes toward homosexuality did not form part of the West's later tradition.

    2. The democratic strand in the classical Mediterranean was not predominant, and its link to the revival of democratic ideas in the late-17th and 18th centuries is almost nonexistent.

3. We cannot deny, however, that some aspects of the classical past would survive or be revived to form part of the Western self-perception.

D. Some common aspects of Christianity raise questions about the boundary lines between the West and the larger Christian world, but defining the West as a civilization is not as problematic as defining Japanese or Russian civilizations. We're skating here between two levels of definitional difficulty: the West seems harder to define as a civilization tradition than India or China but easier than certain cases where imitation was even more rampant.

III. An argument can be made that the postclassical period is where we find some distinctive features that become demonstrably and durably Western.

A. The West was defined by Roman Catholic Christianity, where we find some of its organizational features.

1. The Western tradition of Christianity posited a certain degree of separation between the religious tradition and political structures.

2. Although these distinctions could be blurred, this separation is different from the East European Christian tradition and Islam.

B. The Western form of feudalism ultimately developed a pre-modern parliamentary tradition.

1. Feudalism was taken to mean that rulers had some obligation to consult with their vassals in making certain crucial decisions, particularly where taxation and budgets were involved.

2. This Western parliamentary tradition appears in Spain, England, and elsewhere by the 13th century and becomes a durable part of Western political structures.

C. A third feature involves the political power and independence of Western merchants in the postclassical period. The West was not the world's commercial or capitalist leader in the postclassical period, but Western merchants were less constrained by political regulation in interregional trade than was the case elsewhere.

D. Some authorities on Western Europe in this period have argued that through Christianity, the West developed a sense of the superiority of man over nature that resulted in a special interest in new technologies.

E. Scholars have posed an interesting argument about a distinctive kind of Western family structure that would emerge at the end of the postclassical period and intensify in the centuries thereafter. In this structure, ordinary people married fairly late, replacing extended family traditions with nuclear families.

F. Are we well served in looking at the postclassical period as a formative one for Western civilization?

    1. This period is one in which some classical traditions were incorporated or reused and in which some activities developed as a result of the imitation of other societies.

    2. In this period, a set of specifically Western themes emerged in a few crucial areas of political, social, and economic relationships that we can trace from this point onward.

IV. Another aspect of the task of positioning the West in the postclassical period involves, again, the process of imitation.

A. In relation to other societies operating in the postclassical period, the West was rather backward. Western civilization did not command great respect in the Islamic world.

B. Many Western leaders in various spheres of activity felt this gap as well, which is why they proved such eager imitators. Westerners frequently traveled to Muslim Spain, the Byzantine Empire, and Egypt and were filled with awe at the standards of living they encountered.

C. This gap also explains why the Crusades had their primary impact on the West: the revelation of the difference in living standards between the West and the Middle East spurred new levels of Western trade and consumption.

D. The Crusades also highlighted the paradox of the West's firm conviction that it possessed essential religious truth but, in virtually every other respect, was a somewhat backward society.

V. The West participated actively in postclassical trade, and this trade increased as Western society gained vigor, particularly from about 900 or 1000 CE onward. But as the West entered increasingly into interregional trade patterns, it did so with two distinct disadvantages.

    A. Some of the goods that were most sought after in the West inevitably depended on Islamic middlemen.

        1. Western traders had to go to Egypt or the eastern Mediterranean to obtain goods from India, China, or the Middle East, which meant an additional price to pay to a series of middlemen.

        2. These middlemen were emissaries of a religion that was viewed as heretical and inferior to Christianity.

    B. The larger problem, however, was a balance-of-payments issue.

        1. The West wanted spices, silks, and other goods from Asia, but Western manufacturing offered almost nothing to world trade.

        2. When Vasco da Gama reached India, he brought with him Western textiles and crude metal products that the Indians were not interested in because their products were much better.

    C. Europe existed in the postclassical world as an increasingly eager but disadvantaged participant in larger Afro-Eurasian patterns. One response was to become enthusiastic imitators of technological and other developments.

VI. Toward the end of the postclassical period, certain occurrences began to create new opportunities for the West.

    A. Regional competitors encountered new difficulties. The Byzantine Empire declined, and Arab political unities were shattered. These developments presented new opportunities to borrow technologies from other societies that could help the West overcome its disadvantages.

        1. From China, at the end of the postclassical period, the West adopted a number of technologies, including the compass and explosive powder.

2. The printing press, initially invented in Korea and China, was brought to Western Europe and put to use by a variety of inventors.

B. Western political capacities began to improve in the last centuries of the postclassical era with the emergence of feudal monarchies.

C. Frequent military conflict also spurred the West's interest in technological developments that had military applications.

D. Textbooks in Western civilization routinely assume that changes in the West in the postclassical centuries were the crucial determinants of later Western activity in the world as a whole. World historians, however, take a slightly more cautious view: new opportunities for imitation and the results in terms of a new world role came first and inspired internal changes in the West that would amplify the Western tradition.

Further Reading:

Peter N. Stearns, *Western Civilization in World History.*

David Landes, *Revolution in Time: Clocks in the Making of the Modern World.*

Christopher Dyer, *An Age of Transition? Economy and Society in England in the Later Middle Ages.*

Questions to Consider:

1. How do the arguments for a Greco-Roman origin for Western civilization compare to those for a postclassical origin?

2. What were the major strengths and weaknesses of Western civilization compared to other major civilizations at the end of the postclassical period?

Lecture Fifteen—Transcript
Western Civilization in World Context

The great Indian leader Gandhi—according to the story, at least—was once asked what he thought about Western civilization. He replied, "I think it would be a very good idea." He presumably was questioning, at the time when he was in a struggle with the British, whether the West was civilized. He presumably was not questioning whether the West was Western. I want to use the discussion today to muse a little bit about Western civilization in the world history context. We'll be focusing on two topics primarily, both of which have a bearing on the West as part of the postclassical world. The first topic is when an identifiable Western tradition can be uncovered and what it consisted of and the second, more focused, involves situating the West in the postclassical world. We've already begun that process last time by talking about Western Europe as one of several imitating societies with some distinctive twists but part of a larger pattern. We'll certainly come back to that notion, but I want to add some issues about particular patterns of Western trade and particular patterns of Western dynamism toward the end of the postclassical period.

The relationship between the history of Western civilization and world history, we've already touched on. It is, frankly, complicated. You can't do both exactly at once. At least, you can't do a full Western civilization program in the framework of world history because the result would be to crowd out other societies or to view other societies either as irrelevant or as worth noting only when they're in contact with the West. We've already seen that world historians really think that's a bad approach. It's almost better to stick to the West itself and not pretend you're dealing with the world as a whole at all.

Today I want to discuss not just the issue of how much "West" one can deal with in a world history program; I want to talk about what I think is a more subtle but also a very real issue involving the Western civilization tradition when looked at through world history, and that's the extent to which the West is sometimes viewed almost un-analytically—as if it's a given that requires no particular thought.

We can begin the discussion by situating the West among certain other kinds of definitional issues we've already evoked. I would argue, for example—and all of this is open to discussion—that it's harder to pinpoint the Western tradition—its origins and its precise characteristics—than it is with regard to China or India. China, obviously, has a tradition that goes back presumably to the Shang dynasty, certainly to the classical period, and it always involves certain elements of the state, Confucianism, certain aspects of technology, tradition, etc. Indian history does not necessarily effectively go back to the first civilization on the subcontinent, Harappan civilization. We don't know about links there, but certainly, once Indian society gets going in the classical period—with the caste system, with Hinduism, with certain characteristic political features—you can start talking about an Indian tradition that's identifiable in its linkage between the classical period and today. They are vastly changed. Neither of these traditions, neither the Chinese nor the Indian, is static, but there's a clear pattern.

Western civilization, it seems to me, is more complicated, partly because of the fall of the Roman Empire in the west. It is, of course, common and justifiable to go back to the classical period in looking for the origins of the Western tradition. Elements are certainly going to be there, either because they persisted despite the fall of Rome or because they were later revived.

There are two problems in looking at the classical period as the origins of the West, and these need to be noted, as well. Problem number one we've emphasized before, but it really bears repeating. It is the extent to which the classical Mediterranean tradition fed not only the West but also a number of other societies—Eastern Europe, quite obviously, and the Arab world, as well. This fact makes it a little bit difficult to pull out exactly what's Western in this tradition. For example, classical Greek and Hellenistic science unquestionably had a lingering influence, an impact that survived the classical period itself, but we've seen that this tradition was actively taken up in the Arab world. In a sense, in the postclassical period, Western science, partly because it copied the Arabs, was really part of a scientific community that was indeed partially derived from Greece and Hellenism but was widely shared and not distinctively Western at all. Later, arguably, the West will produce a more decisively different scientific tradition, but at this point, frankly, it's a bit hard to pull out.

The same thing holds to the great debate between rationalism and faith. This was a debate that turns out to have been shared in the postclassical period in Islam and in Western Christianity alike. Interestingly, it was not a debate that particularly affected Eastern Christianity. In other words, there's heritage to the classical tradition; unquestionably, it's not always distinctively Western.

The second problem in overemphasizing the classical origins of a Western strand involves how much of the classical tradition did not survive or at least did not survive in any direct sense. Take a simple but not insignificant example: Classical Greek and Roman attitudes toward homosexuality did not form part of the West's later tradition with regard to homosexuality. There's a very different pattern. Whether the pattern emerged at the outset of Christianity or only later in the postclassical period has been debated, but there's simply no classical connection to characteristic Western attitudes toward homosexuality, insofar as this forms a part, if a subterranean part, of the Western tradition.

Here, I'm going to be very candid: I'm editorializing a little bit. Take that staple of American education, the notion that the West's democratic tradition goes back to Greece and Rome. Athens had a democracy. It's not exactly the modern form of democracy, but that's quibbling. It was a democracy. Rome had a subordinate democratic element in its Republican constitution, although its main emphasis was on aristocratic rule. Unquestionably, there is a democratic strand in the classical Mediterranean past. It was not the predominant strand, but it was there. Unquestionably, also, by the time one gets to the late 17th, 18th centuries and Western thinkers are beginning to think about democracy again, they will hark back to the Greco-Roman example. I don't think this caused their thinking, but it certainly provided some rhetorical cover. In that sense, there is a tiny bit of connection, but we're talking about a gap of almost 2,000 years between the classical instance of democracy and anything such as the contemporary Western one. Where's the filler? Where's the connection? Frankly, there isn't much. Democratic ideas appear in the West almost not at all in the postclassical period. There is a brief possibility in one popular rising in Rome in which classical traditions may have been still evoked and remembered, but the notion of a Western strand of democracy stretching from the classical period to the present, I think, is, at the very least, highly debatable. In my view, it's a nonstarter; it's a historical distortion. It's understandable because it lets us think that this political system we value today has these really venerable roots, but it just doesn't work.

If the classical period raises two crucial kinds of questions about Western origin, what are the options? Nobody's denying, by the way, that some segments of the classical past would survive or be revived and would form part of the Western self-perception. To take another tact, I don't think that defining the Western tradition, defining the West as a civilization, is as problematic as, say, defining Japanese or Russian civilizations—issues we talked about in our previous discussion. Japan raises huge questions about whether it should be seen as a separate entity as a civilization or as part of a larger, Chinese-influenced East Asian whole. That issue does not clearly arise for the Western case. It's true, of course, that one needs to think about some common aspects to Christianity, which would raise questions about the boundary lines between the West and the larger Christian whole. But, generally, it seems to me that most historians have been reasonably comfortable in arguing that the marked divisions between West and East European versions of Christianity—which were sort of ratified and solidified in the 11th century with the Great Schism between East and West—these divisions in doctrine, in church organization, in church-state relationships, in religious and artistic traditions, and in philosophical traditions make it fairly clear that the Western tradition is not Christianity as a whole but a subset of it, initially obviously organized primarily by the Roman Catholic Church.

We're skating here between two levels of definitional difficulty. My argument is that the West is harder to define as a civilization tradition than India or China or maybe even the Middle East but easier than certain cases where imitation was even more rampant, as in the Japanese instance or, possibly, the Russian.

I would argue—and this brings us back to the period we're examining, more generally—that it's in the postclassical period specifically that one really finds some distinctive features that become demonstrably Western and fairly durably so. Although, of course, they, too, will change over time, just as is true with any civilization tradition. If this is so, what are these features? Let me suggest three or four. First, in the postclassical period, obviously, the West was defined by Roman Catholic Christianity. So there were, in that particular version of Christianity, the origins of some distinctive Western features, and there was also an organizational basis that one can look to, as well. Obviously, the Western tradition of Christianity posited a certain degree of separation between a distinct church institution, a distinct religious tradition, and political structures. Now, these distinctions could be blurred. In point of fact, states often muscled in on the church and the church often muddied its own waters by calling on state aid when it might have been better suited to try to solve its own problems by itself. But the notions of a distinctive version of Christianity and a partial separation between a religious sphere and a political sphere strike me as one element in, what one might call, an emerging Western tradition—different, obviously, from the East European Christian tradition but different from Islam and other parts of Asia, as well.

Second component: The postclassical period, through the particular Western form of feudalism and its dominant political system, not immediately but ultimately, developed a clear, if at this point pre-modern, parliamentary tradition. Feudalism was ultimately taken to mean that rulers had something of an obligation to consult with their vassals and, possibly, other elements of their constituency in making certain crucial decisions, particularly where taxation and budgets were involved. This parliamentary tradition, which flowed out of Western feudalism, didn't result from Japanese feudalism, which had a rather different if equally important later heritage. This Western parliamentary tradition shows up in Spain, in England, and elsewhere by the 13th century and becomes a durable part of Western political structures most of the time thereafter. There are other traditions in others parts of the world that also involve consultation with councils. One doesn't want to overdo this distinctiveness, but along with church-state relations in Western Christianity, I would posit this as at least a possible defining piece.

A third component—and this one needs to be stated particularly carefully—involves the political power and independence of Western merchants as their traditions emerged in the postclassical period, as well. The care here needs to be directed toward emphasizing that the West was not the world's commercial leader in the postclassical period. It wasn't even necessarily a leader in capitalism. Islam had a great deal more capitalism than the West did at this point. What I'm arguing here is that as Western merchants began to gain [greater] dynamism, participating in trade throughout various sectors of Europe and then even in interregional trade, their vigor, their commercial activity was less constrained by political regulation than would be true in the Middle East or China. These were other centers of actually more sophisticated merchant activity but where state regulation and state supervision were more present, as well.

Here, then, are three possibilities. Others might add a couple of additional [ones]. In addition to church and church-state, parliament, and a particular sphere of independence from merchants, some authorities on Western Europe in this period have argued that Christianity helped the West generate a particular sense of the superiority of man over nature that would make the West particularly interested in new technologies—not, at this point, a world technological leader—but particularly interested in new technologies either of their own invention or as they could be borrowed from other societies. This is at least worth thinking about.

Finally, although this one actually developed more clearly a bit later on, there's an interesting argument about a distinctive kind of Western family structure that would emerge beginning at the end of the postclassical period and then intensifying in the later centuries. [This was] a family structure in which ordinary people married fairly late, thus having an emphasis on nuclear families, husband-wife families, in which wives and husbands had to collaborate or conflict particularly directly that contrasted with the extended family traditions that described actually most of the rest of the world, one way or another. Here's another interesting Western ingredient, a less expected one, that might be worked into a definition of Western origins.

The first issue, then, involves the possibility that we are well served in looking at the postclassical period as really a formative one for Western civilization. It is one in which certain classical traditions could be incorporated or reutilized. It is one in which certain activities developed simply as a result of imitation of other societies, but it's also one in which, in a few crucial areas of political, social, and economic relationships, something of a set of Western themes is beginning to emerge that we can trace from that point onward, just as we can trace Indian or Chinese traditions even earlier on.

The second aspect of positioning the West in the postclassical period is, in one sense, an easier one. We started the process, again, by talking about the West as an imitator. Obviously, if you look at the West in relationship to the other societies operating in the postclassical period, the West was long a rather backward society. Muslims, who were not necessarily totally intolerant of Christianity, tended to look on West Europeans as clumsy, unsophisticated, and possibly, good warriors. It's somewhat of a football-player image of Western society that we perhaps have retained traces of even today. This was not a Western civilization that commanded great respect in Islam—the Muslims were being unfair, just as we've returned the favor in more recent periods—but the sense of a serious civilization gap was perceptible and, to some extent, defensible in terms of the West's position in world affairs. Obviously, many Western leaders in various spheres of activity felt this gap directly, as well. This is why, among other things, they proved such eager imitators. This is why they frequently traveled to other places in Muslim Spain, in the Byzantine Empire, and in Egypt and were filled with awe at the standards of living, at the urban cultures, they encountered there. This is why the Crusades—obviously, in a burst of a sense of religious superiority and obligation, called to urge Western leaders to retake the Holy Land from Islam—this is why the Crusades actually ended up having their primary impact on the West, as a revelation of the gap between Western living standards and those of the Middle East [and] as a spur to new levels of Western trade and Western consumption.

Western society in the postclassical period [was] poised, I think, somewhat uneasily, between a firm conviction—sometimes pressed to the point of absolute cruel intolerance—that this was a society that possessed essential religious truth as no other society did, on the one hand. On the other, [the West had] a nagging sense that despite this religious superiority, in virtually every other aspect, this society was somewhat backward, somewhat lagging.

The West also faced a particular issue that we need to discuss a little bit today and then come back to as we go back to a larger world schema. We've seen, and it's quite obvious, that the West participated actively in postclassical trade. This activity increased as Western society gained vigor, particularly from about 900 or 1000 CE onward. Western merchant activity pressed into the Mediterranean. Italian ships, particularly from Venice and Genoa, began to carry trade actively in the Mediterranean, ferrying passengers and goods from Islamic societies, as well as from the West itself. The West entered increasingly into interregional trade patterns, but it did so with two obvious disadvantages. The first is fairly well known but deserves emphasis. That was the extent to which, for some of the goods that were most sought after in the West from interregional trade, it inevitably depended on Islamic middlemen. Western traders had to go to Egypt or to the eastern Mediterranean in order to seek the goods that would come from India, from China, or the Middle East. This meant, quite simply in terms of economics, an additional price to pay to an additional series of middlemen, but even more, it meant the necessity of dealing with emissaries of a religion that was viewed as heretical and inferior to Christianity—an awkward cultural position, as well as a slightly awkward economic one.

The bigger problem, however, was what in modern parlance we would call a balance-of-payments issue. The West wanted goods from various parts of Asia. It wanted spices; it wanted silks; etc. What was it to use to pay for these goods? Western manufacturing offered almost nothing to world trade. It was a manufacturing system that improved during the postclassical period itself. Textile products became better. New kinds of woolens were introduced. Within the Western sphere itself, there were clear manufacturing gains, but this was simply not world-class manufacturing. The West had no distinctive minerals or agricultural products to offer. There was a little bit of gold available and the West had some silver resources, but it was not nearly as well endowed in this regard as, say, Africa was. The West faced an obvious dilemma. It wanted goods that it had difficulty paying for in terms of the strengths of the Western economy itself. This is strictly slightly after the postclassical period itself, but it carries the themes onward that I am discussing here. A revealing moment occurred when the Portuguese explorer Vasco da Gama rounded the southern tip of Africa and reached India in 1498–99. He brought with him on this first trip some Western textile goods—woolens that the Indians didn't want; they had much better textiles—he brought some crude metal pots and products. The Indians didn't want those. They had much better metal products. He happily did bring some gold. This they did like, and this allowed him to purchase enough to take Indian products back to Portugal and persuade the king that a regular series of voyages would be desirable in the future. Without the gold, he would have been lost. As we will discuss later, when he went back the second time, he had a remedy, but it was not a remedy that reflected any particular European economic gains.

Europe, then, existed in the postclassical world as an increasingly eager participant in larger Afro-Eurasian patterns but a participant at some disadvantage, either because of the greater recency of cultural and political and economic achievements or because of [its] basic resource position or both. One response—and this is clearly emerging in the postclassical period itself—was to become particularly eager imitators of developments, particularly technological developments, elsewhere. Here, to a real extent, the West would luck out. Toward the end of the postclassical period, two things happened that began to create new opportunities for the West.

In the first place, regional competitors—particularly the Byzantine Empire [and], to a lesser degree, the Arabs—encountered some new difficulties. Arab political unities shattered. The Byzantine Empire declined increasingly, to the extent that Western trips actually raided Constantinople during the Fourth Crusade. This may have relaxed some of the tension on Western Europe, but the more important point was that new opportunities arose to borrow major new technologies from other societies that could help the West, over time, answer the question: How do we get out of this fix? How do we more clearly match our sense of religious superiority to our relationships with our neighbors? How do we resolve the balance-of-payment problems in ways that will allow us to participate more successfully, more freely in larger world trade?

The imitation opportunities occurred vis-à-vis the Middle East. From the Middle East, we've seen that the West eagerly borrowed a number of technological and cultural devices, but opportunities also opened up in new Western connections with China. From China, at the end of the postclassical period, the West would take a number of technological items. The compass we mentioned before, but the great one was explosive powder, invented by the Chinese and used by them for military purposes but on a somewhat limited scale. The West would learn about explosive powder, would adopt it as their own, and would, by the early 14th century, begin to add formally made guns and cannon to the utilization of this powder in ways that differed from Chinese patterns. The second great borrowing utilized a little later was, of course, the printing press, initially invented in

Korea and China, carried to Western Europe during this same late-postclassical period, and put to use by a variety of inventors, but particularly Gutenberg in 1450, at the end of the period in question.

It's always possible to look at the West at the end of the postclassical period, at a point where the West is on the verge of beginning to assert a new and more active world role. It's always possible to look at internal developments in the West itself. Quite clearly, Western political capacities were beginning to improve in the last centuries in the postclassical era with the emergence of feudal monarchies. Very clearly, military rivalries in the West—the frequency of war, the frequency of feudal conflict or conflict among monarchies—helped spur the West's interest particularly in technological developments, either imported or homegrown, that had military implications.

Christian inspiration in the Crusades—or, later, in Spain and Portugal as they chased the Muslims out during the later stages of the postclassical period—Christian missionary inspiration might inspire the West to new levels of activity. Early facets of the Renaissance, presumably a new spirit in Western cultural affairs, might inspire new Western activity onward. There's no question that textbooks in Western civilization routinely assume that changes within the West, in the later postclassical centuries leading to the Renaissance, were the crucial determinants of later Western activity in the world as a whole. But a world historian, I think, can legitimately—and I don't think this is an anti-Western stance—take a slightly more cautious view. Possibly, new opportunities for imitation and the results in terms of a new world role actually came first and then helped inspire changes internally in the West that would amplify the Western tradition, that would build on it in ways that become familiar parts of the Western story.

Lecture Sixteen
The Mongol Years

Scope:

World history between the early-13th and the mid-14th centuries was dominated by the conquests of the Mongols. The Mongols, a nomadic people from Central Asia, began a conquest of China early in the 13th century. Within a few decades, an interlocking network of Mongol empires, or *khanates*, stretched from China in the east to western Russia, embracing a significant part of the Middle East and pressing into Southeast Asia, while organizing much of the Mongol heartland in Central Asia. Mongols were regarded as bloodthirsty conquerors; they could make cruel examples of civilian populations who tried to hold out against their attacks. But this bad press also reflected the resentments of conquered peoples such as the Russians and Chinese. World history has rehabilitated the Mongols significantly. Once their rule was established, they could prove tolerant and even enlightened; they certainly did not press subject peoples to abandon existing cultures or local institutions. More important, the Mongol network greatly accelerated travel and contacts between Asia and Europe, to the primary advantage of the latter. It was under the Mongols that such travelers as Marco Polo brought back information about China and specific access to Chinese technologies, including printing and explosive powder. The Mongol period was short-lived—beginning to fade by the later-14th century— but its impact, particularly in technology exchange, continued to affect world history. This is the context that prompted *The Economist*, in 1999, to name Chinggis Khan the most important historical figure of the then-closing millennium in world history.

Outline

I. The Mongol era in world history covered much of the 13th and 14th centuries and had decisive results for most of the societies in Europe and Asia.

A. The traditional view of the Mongols as bloodthirsty barbarians has been almost completely reassessed. More recently, the Mongols have been seen as an unusually tolerant people who established a political system that facilitated interregional contact to a greater extent than had ever been possible in world history.

B. In 1999, *The Economist*, a respectable British periodical, named Chinggis Khan the man of the millennium. This was largely a tribute to Chinggis as the first in a succession of Mongol rulers who would administer their conquests reasonably wisely and would use conquest deliberately to accelerate contact among different peoples.

C. It is true that the Mongols could be cruel, killing urban civilians to ensure that others would yield more quickly to their forces. Nonetheless, the dominant revisionist picture seems valid.

II. The Mongol invasion of China was the last in a series of eruptions from the nomadic territories of Central Asia that had earlier seen such groups as the Indo-Europeans and Huns pour out.

A. Probably some combination of population pressure in a fairly fragile nomadic economy, political rivalries, and divisions in China itself prompted the Mongols to eye the rich society to their east. The Mongols had long been one of several border people harassing the Chinese and pressing into Chinese territory during the Song dynasty.

B. Early in the 13th century, Chinggis Khan conquered a good bit of China. The conquest was completed in ensuing decades, so that Chinggis's grandson, Kublai Khan, became ruler of China. This Mongol rule, known as the Yuan dynasty, would last for most of the next century.

C. Once in power, the Mongols made use of the Chinese government system and bureaucracy, along with Confucian values. Although they disapproved of many aspects of Chinese culture, they were generally tolerant.

D. Mongol rule in China brought clear economic benefits, expanding both manufacturing and trade opportunities.

E. In addition to Chinese bureaucrats, the Mongols used a variety of foreign administrators in a deliberate attempt to open up the society to a wider set of influences.

III. Mongol conquest soon branched out from China.

    A. In the eastern part of the Middle East, the Mongols conquered Baghdad and overthrew the last Arab caliphate. A Mongol khanate was established in the eastern Middle East which held sway for several decades. Mongol khanates also fanned out in Central Asia, aiding in the first coherent political organization of that region.

    B. The other great conquest of the Mongols involved Russia toward the end of the 13th century. In Russia, rulers were having increasing difficulties with restive nobles. The resulting Mongol sweep across European Russia exempted very few territories but spared Western Europe.

    C. Mongol efforts also pressed into Southeast Asia at key points.

    D. By the late-13th century, the block of territory held by interlocking Mongol khanates was without precedent in world history.

IV. The results of these invasions were significant, with some durable elements.

    A. Overland travel from west to east became increasingly easy.

        1. Popes began to send Christian emissaries to the Mongols quite early, both to persuade the invaders to stay out of Western Europe and Catholic territory and to convert some peoples in the Mongol realms.

        2. Western merchants took advantage of the safe passage granted by khans into Mongol territory.

        3. We also know of some trips by European Jews, artists, and entertainers.

    B. This openness amplified exchanges of knowledge that would gradually begin to close the traditional technology gap between East Asia and Western Europe.

    C. Accelerated contact in this period also had a downside. It was in the Mongol period that the Black Death began in China and spread quickly to the Middle East and Europe.

        1. One-quarter to one-third of the population of Western Europe and the Middle East succumbed to the plague.

2. The advantages of access to new technology may have outweighed the drawbacks of this level of mortality in Western Europe.

V. Mongol rule began to decline in the latter part of the 14th century.

  A. The Mongols were unsuccessful in two efforts at invading Japan by sea, suggesting some limits to their capacity for expansion.,

  B. The Chinese began to organize more effectively against Mongol rule, ousted the Mongols in the latter part of the 14th century, and quickly established the Ming dynasty.

  C. Mongol rule in Russia ended later.

   1. Early in the 15th century, local Russian rulers increasingly asserted their independence.

   2. By 1450, an autonomous Russian area was established in the Moscow region, which then became the center of Russia.

  D. The expulsion of the Mongols from China and Russia led to reactions that indicated the distaste that these peoples felt for Mongol control.

   1. The Chinese would become preoccupied with creating systems to prevent the return of invaders like the Mongols—including the reconstruction of the Great Wall of China.

   2. The Russian reaction was to undertake a steady series of conquests, initially designed to push the Mongols farther back but ultimately becoming a durable Russian commitment to expansionism.

  E. The end of the Mongol period for world history meant a return to increasing political barriers; the opportunities for overland travel between Europe and China receded for a considerable period of time.

VI. The Mongol period should be viewed as something of a rebalancing among major societies in Europe and Asia.

  A. The impact on China:

1. The Chinese hostility toward outsiders deepened, and defensive barriers were created to prevent future invasion.

2. The Mongols had also confirmed China's importance in world manufacturing.

B. The impact on Russia:

1. Russians turned from a regional people to an increasingly aggressive and expansionist people.

2. This would be a major theme of the next period in world history and continues to some extent even today.

C. The impact on Japan:

1. The Japanese, having faced two Mongol invasions and been spared in one case by a typhoon that destroyed the Mongol fleet, began to think of themselves as superior to China.

2. This sense of Japanese isolation would be an interesting factor in world history in the succeeding period.

D. The impact on Western Europe:

1. Aside from borderline clashes, Western Europe did not experience the cost or anxiety of direct Mongol invasion; instead, it received the benefit of unusually free contact with Asia.

2. The Europeans saw the advantages that new kinds of weaponry could bring to a highly militaristic society.

3. The Europeans would make use of printing in ways that would have deep implications for their culture and bureaucracy.

4. The Europeans, in other words, were the leading beneficiaries from this Mongol era.

E. The impact on Sub-Saharan Africa:

1. Sub-Saharan Africa experienced no particular impact from the Mongol conquests, but at the same time it had no stimulus to learn from new technological opportunities.

2. This was a null case, in other words, that would contrast interestingly with the experience of Western Europe.

VII. The decline of the Mongol system could have overwhelmed the pattern of intensifying interregional contacts that we have so vigorously emphasized for the postclassical period, but this system was so successful in its larger sense that it readily survived the Mongols.

  A. The question at the end of the 14th century was not whether world contacts would recede, but rather what system, with what routes and under whose sponsorship, would replace the Mongol system?

  B. The Mongol era briefly replaced and extended the system created earlier by the Arabs, but it was not the last gasp of global interconnections. That chapter was about to reopen in new ways in the 15th century.

Further Reading:

Gerard Chaliand, *Nomadic Empires: From Mongolia to the Danube.*

Jack Weatherford, *Genghis Khan and the Making of the Modern World.*

Thomas Allsen, *Culture and Conquest in Mongol Eurasia.*

Questions to Consider:

1. Is the shift in evaluation of the Mongols historically appropriate, or does it suggest a troubling change in contemporary values toward more tolerance for bloodthirsty conquest?

2. Looking at Afro-Eurasia overall, which societies benefited, which societies were disadvantaged, and which societies were unaffected by the Mongol conquests?

Lecture Sixteen—Transcript
The Mongol Years

We're talking in this session about an extraordinary period in world history that covers much of the 13th and 14th centuries, 100–150 years. This is a period that [is] known now as the Mongol era or interlude in world history. It had some decisive results for most of the societies in Europe and Asia, although the results differed from one case to the next. I can't think of a people that have been so reconstituted in the historical view as have been the Mongols in the last decade or so. When I took history, if the Mongols were mentioned at all, it was with a grimace and an apology because they were bloodthirsty barbarians who killed a lot of people to no purpose whatsoever. More recently, the Mongols can be seen as an unusually tolerant people who managed to establish a political system that facilitated interregional contact to a greater extent than had ever before been possible—or would be possible for some time later—in world history. It's a decisive interlude in which the general theme of interregional contact was directly intensified and furthered in ways that, in broad outline, would survive the Mongol period itself—though we need to come back to this at the end of the discussion today.

In 1999, the *Economist Magazine*, a respectable, rather conservative British periodical, named Chinggis Khan the man of the millennium, an extraordinary accolade. Think of all the other candidates. This was probably partly due to his military achievements. Here was a nomadic leader who managed to defeat much of one of the great civilizations in history at the time, the Chinese. But it was really more a tribute to Chinggis as the first of a succession of Mongol rulers who would manage to administer conquest reasonably wisely and who would use conquest deliberately to accelerate the contact among different kinds of people. Whether he deserves the honor or not, frankly, is immaterial. I think the notion of choosing *the* man or *the* person of a 1,000-year span is a little silly. I would want at least three choices, personally. But the revision is striking. The Mongols have now, if anything, a revered place in world history, in contrast to the dustbin to which they'd been traditionally relegated.

Probably, as in any revision, this one may have pressed a bit too far. The Mongols could be cruel. Chinggis Khan could kill urban civilians in order to set examples to other cities, so they would yield more quickly to his forces. After all, the Mongols did not have a terribly numerous army and they needed to use devices of intimidation to bolster their chances of success. Undoubtedly, Mongol rulers subsequently were not only seen as disruptive and terrifying but could be disruptive and terrifying. Certainly, that was the widespread impression among Russians, as Mongol invasions penetrated that society. We don't need to whitewash the slate entirely. There are downsides to the Mongol experience, but—and here we may perhaps not pay sufficient attention to casualties and cruelties of the past—the dominant revisionist picture does seem valid. This was an important episode in world history that furthered connections in ways that had durable results and, to some extent, began a process of reshuffling among major societies in ways that would have durable consequences, as well.

We don't know precisely why the Mongols decided to invade China. This was, in one sense, the last—and it was the last—of a series of eruptions from the nomadic territories of Central Asia that had earlier seen groups such as the Indo-Europeans [and] the Huns pour out. Probably some combination of population pressure in a nomadic economy that was fairly fragile and political rivalries, which were undoubtedly involved in the immediate environment of Chinggis Khan, encouraged the Mongols to look to the rich society to their east and divisions in China itself. The Mongols had long been one of several border people who were harassing the Chinese and pressing into what was traditionally Chinese territory during the Song dynasty. Probably opportunities, in terms of Chinese imperial decline, encouraged the process, as well.

In any event, early in the 13th century, Chinggis Khan did invade China and conquered a good bit of it. The conquest was completed in ensuing decades, so that his grandson, the great Kublai Khan—the Khan that Marco Polo encountered if, indeed, he went to China—the great Kublai Khan was ruler of China entire, and this Mongol rule in China, known in Chinese as the Yuan dynasty, would last for the better part of the ensuing century. In China, the Mongols occupied a really interesting and distinctive position. They used the Chinese government system. They used Confucian values and they used the Chinese bureaucracy, even though many bureaucrats resented them greatly. The Mongols were—once in power, at least—tolerant. They saw the advantage of not overturning established systems. They didn't insist on identifying their own ways and ramming them down people's throats. The Mongols did, however, actually disapprove of many aspects of Chinese values. They found Chinese court life stultifying and continued to live in tents outside capital cities. They didn't like the Chinese gender system. Mongols were among the nomadic peoples—and nomads varied greatly in this regard—who gave women a considerable voice in political decision-making. The wife of Kublai Khan was instrumental in calming him down on occasion and urging that he adopt restraint toward Chinese traditions. But, no question, the Mongols thought that foot binding and the subjugation of women in the postclassical Chinese fashion was a bad thing.

The Chinese reciprocated by coming to detest the Mongols with that kind of resentment that combines disdain for barbarian, unwashed peoples—I don't personally know Mongol bathing-habits; the stereotype was probably pressed too far—but it was the combination of disdain for a people viewed as inferior who nevertheless had decisive power. The Chinese would work assiduously to throw this new dynasty out, which they accomplished toward the end of the 14th century, but actually Mongol rule in China brought clear economic benefits. Chinese manufacturing developed further. Chinese opportunities to trade with other parts of the world expanded. Indeed, the Mongols intensified the kind of Chinese relationship to the world network that we have seen developed earlier in the Song dynasty prior to the Mongol incursion.

In China, the Mongols utilized—along with Chinese bureaucrats—a variety of foreign peoples. This was a regime that was deliberately hoping to open up the societies it ruled to a wider set of influences. Christians from Western Europe were welcomed. Marco Polo and his uncles were presumably used in Mongol administration—they had learned the Mongol language earlier, though they never learned Chinese. People from Persia were widely used. Nestorian Christians, a Christian branch that had long since migrated out of the Middle East, were used and their places of worship newly tolerated. This was an interesting mix of successful adaptation of Chinese customs and a type of welcome mat to peoples from other societies. The net result, clearly, was trade benefits for China itself—even though this did not overcome Chinese hostility—and a new openness to China for peoples in a whole host of other places—including, of course, Western Europe itself.

Mongol conquest soon surpassed the conquest of China. We've discussed earlier the importance of the Mongol invasion of the eastern part of the Middle East, where they conquered Baghdad and overthrew the last Arab caliphate. A Mongol khanate was established in the eastern Middle East, including Persia, which held sway for several decades. Mongol khanates fanned out in Central Asia. For the first time, Central Asia became somewhat coherently politically organized. The other great conquest of the Mongols involved Russia toward the end of the 13th century. Just as with the Middle East and the Mongol's success in overturning the caliphate, where earlier Arab political divisions—increasingly, unsuccessful efforts at caliphate rule—helped prepare a successful invasion, well before the Mongol invasion of Russia, Russian rulers were having increasing difficulties with restive nobles. They were having problems maintaining the coherence of the Russian territory. As is so often the case in history, successful invasion, in this instance, combined with prior internal weakness. But the result was a tremendous Mongol sweep across European Russia, exempting only a very few territories, interestingly stopping short of pressing beyond the boundaries of Eastern Europe, thus sparing Western Europe and creating a new kind of division between the Russian experience and that of most of the rest of Europe. It was a division between direct Mongol rule and a good bit of anxiety but, frankly, ultimate freedom from this kind of invading pressure.

Mongol efforts also pressed into Southeast Asia at key points. There are no really durable conquests involved, but this was brought into the Mongol horizon to some degree. By the late 13th century, in what is one of the most amazing sweeps of successful invasions in world history—perhaps, the most amazing—Mongol rule had established khanates, interlocking khanates tied by blood relations and cultural affiliations, from China in the east all the way to western Russia in the west, from northern China and Russia in the north to the Middle East and incursions into Southeast Asia in the south—a block of territory that simply had no precedent in world history.

The results are familiar and important. It became increasingly easy to travel back and forth overland from west to east and east to west. European travelers were obviously particularly important. Popes began to send Christian emissaries to the Mongols quite early with two purposes in mind, initially. The biggest goal was defensive. Papal emissaries wanted to persuade the Mongols to stay out of Western Europe and Catholic territory. But gradually, there emerged some hope that religious missions might convert some peoples in the Mongol realms, including in China, and make contacts with small Christian groups in these regions, as well. Not a lot happened in that regard, but a number of papal emissaries went, and some increased knowledge of China resulted from these trips, as well. The more famous trips—including, of course, the travels of the Polos—involved Western merchants, particularly from Italy, although there were French and others, as well. They involved Western merchants who went to the Mongol realms, taking advantage of the safe passage that the khans could grant. You could enter one khan's territory and get passage that would ensure you favorable protection as you went onward. Although we know of only a few of these trips—and, again, the Polos were particularly important, but there were trips by a few European Jews and others, as well—the result actually uncovers a surprising number of Europeans who made it to China for one reason or another. There were European artists established in China and European entertainers. The opportunity to see a new place, possibly earn money in a new place, and have a different kind of experience was clearly widely stimulating.

The consequences amplified, of course, the kinds of knowledge that exchanges had already been bringing to the world network. It was during this period that Europeans had a particularly clear opportunity to learn about Chinese technologies and to import some of them directly. They learned about some that they didn't take full advantage of; for example, Marco Polo describes the use of coal as well as charcoal in smelting iron in ways that wouldn't be widely taken over in Europe for some time. But key Chinese developments, particularly printing and explosive powder, were crucial imports that passed west from the east at this point in time. Gradually, this would begin to create a process in which the huge traditional technology gap between East Asia and Western Europe would begin to be somewhat closed. That, perhaps, is one of the crucial long-term results of this process.

Contacts also, as they accelerated in this period, had a downside. It was in the Mongol period that the Black Death began in China and spread quickly to the Middle East and Europe. The bubonic plague presumably—although there's some debate about this—began in the Gobi Desert in western China, passed quickly into eastern China, and then, because of the trade connections between China and other parts of the world, spread rapidly elsewhere. Bubonic plague began to be registered in Middle Eastern port cities by the middle of the 14th century and in Western European cities a couple of decades thereafter. In both these cases, death rates were appallingly high. Upwards of a quarter to a third of the population of Western Europe and the Middle East succumbed to the bubonic plague in a major population blow that would obviously have crucial effects on these societies thereafter. On balance, at least in the West European case, while the population blow was huge and had major dislocating effects in wage relationships [and] labor relationships and major implications as well for religious retreat against this wrath of God, interestingly, West European dynamism was not as significantly dented by this population blow as might have been imagined. It's possible to suggest that the pluses of access to new technology may actually have outweighed the drawbacks of this level of mortality, though both factors would weigh on the European experience, not just at this point but for many decades and even centuries thereafter.

Mongol rule began to decline in the later part of the 14th century. The Mongols were unsuccessful in two efforts at invading Japan by sea. While this was not necessarily a catastrophic setback, it did suggest some clear limits to the Mongol capacity to expand further. Most clearly, the Chinese began to organize more effectively against Mongol rule and chased the Mongols out in the latter part of the 14th century, quickly establishing a new dynastic cycle within China with the advent of the Ming dynasty—one of the dynasties that tended to crop up after a crisis period and then could enjoy, as the Ming did, many decades of subsequent success.

Mongol rule in Russia ended later. The Mongols had operated in Russia, as well as in China, fairly tolerantly. They didn't insist on, for example, conversions away from Christianity. They levied taxes on the Russians, but they didn't interfere intensively in Russian administration. But the Russians unquestionably viewed the Mongol period as an outside tyranny. Indeed, perhaps because of previous Russian decline, the Mongol rule did not bring the economic benefits to Russia that it did to China. This was not a vibrant society under Mongol sway. But early in the 15th century, particularly around the duchy of Moscow, local Russian rulers began to assert increasing independence from the Mongols. By 1450—ending the postclassical period in the Russian case—they began to establish an autonomous Russian area in the Moscow region, which then became the center of Russia from that time onward, somewhat eastward from the Russian centers during the postclassical period.

The expulsion of the Mongols from China and then from Russia led to interesting subsequent reactions, both of which indicated the distaste that these peoples had felt for Mongol control, but which pointed in rather different directions. The Chinese would obviously be preoccupied, not just with chasing the Mongols out, but with creating systems that might prevent their return. The most coherent expression of this was the beginning of the dramatic reconstruction of the Great Wall of China to the form that it takes today. The Chinese wall previously had been an earthen works wall. This wall was brick. It allowed massive patrols to operate on its surface—a huge, huge investment to seclude China from this direction of barbarian invasion. Partly because Russia was less protected by natural frontiers, Russian reaction was more in terms of a steady series of conquests initially designed to push the Mongols farther and farther back, but a series that would turn into a durable Russian commitment to expansionism, a reaction in some ways rather similar to the Chinese. In both cases, you want to do something that will prevent this dreadful occupation from recurring, but which pointed specifically in quite opposite directions. It was defensive in the one instance; expansionist and aggressive in the other. This, obviously, would enter historical channels in subsequent periods in world history, as well.

The end of the Mongol period for world history more generally meant a return to increasing political barriers, including just sheer brigandage. It's important to realize that when we talk glibly about interregional travel and trade without political controls, one of the huge barriers to regular contact and one of the huge costs of the whole system was the frequency with which bandits could beset groups of travelers, particularly in overland cases, but also on the seas. Overland travel became less possible. The opportunities to use overland travel to reach between Europe and China actually receded considerably for quite a good period of time. The specific facilities that the Mongol period had offered came to an end, but there were further repercussions. The Mongol period needs to be seen as something of a rebalancing among major societies in Europe and in Asia. The impact on China was considerable but, in many ways, somewhat fleeting. The Chinese perhaps deepened their hostility toward outsiders. They certainly, as I've already indicated, created defensive reactions designed to prevent this from happening in the future. But the Mongols had also confirmed China's importance in world manufacturing, and the Chinese would continue to enjoy this position for many centuries. Therefore, this was an important modification of the Chinese stance but not a fundamental disruption. The long-term Mongol impact on Russia was, as I've really already suggested, more considerable in turning the Russians from a somewhat regional people to an increasingly aggressive and expansionist people. This would be a major theme of the next period in world history and continues to be some preoccupation even today.

The Mongols had an interesting impact on Japan. The Japanese, having faced two Mongol invasions and having been spared in one case because of a typhoon that destroyed the Mongol fleet—the Japanese referred to this as a "divine wind"—began to think that perhaps they were not only, along with China, the pinnacle of world civilization, but perhaps they were the pinnacle of world civilization even aside from China. After all, the Mongols had taken China; they didn't take Japan. So a Japanese sense of isolation from, and superiority to, much of the rest of the world and newly applying this even to relationships to China would be an interesting factor in world history in the succeeding period.

Mongol impact on Western Europe was obviously decisive. The Europeans simply lucked out. I don't think there's any other way to play it. This was just one of those fortunate accidents in world history that one needs to acknowledge sometimes occur. The Europeans lucked out. The Mongols didn't invade them at all. They [Europeans] got a little scared. There were some borderline clashes in Hungary and elsewhere, but they did not have the cost or anxiety of direct invasion. The fear abated fairly quickly, as well. What they did get was the benefit of this century of unusually free contact with Asia, unusual opportunities to import Asian technologies, and they used this to the hilt. As indicated, the Europeans, whatever their other faults or virtues, turned out to be an excessively zealous imitating people at this point. They knew a good thing when they saw one. They knew the advantages that new kinds of weaponry could bring in a society that was highly militaristic, in which each local ruler, each local feudal monarch, was interested in whatever advantage could be obtained. The Europeans took to Chinese explosive powder exceedingly quickly and adapted it to new metallurgical techniques that allowed the manufacture of guns and cannon, so that the explosive force could be more clearly directed and targeted. They would make use of printing, as well, in ways that would have deep implications for European culture and bureaucracy. The Europeans, in other words, clearly were the leading beneficiaries from this Mongol era, perhaps benefiting in part because of their own alertness to the possibilities of imitation. You don't want to withdraw a European attribute here, but they were beneficiaries also of a simple concatenation of forces that has to be termed just good luck.

It would be stretching it to apply the Mongol experience to other societies, but I do want to mention one other case because we'll return to it in a session quite soon. Sub-Saharan Africa had no particular impact from the Mongol experience one way or another. African goods did reach the Mongols. This was part of the long-distance trading patterns. Certain African animal products were used as decorations by Mongol rulers, but the African experience itself was not significantly affected. Africa continued to deal with the rest of the world mainly through the medium of Islamic traders, and these traders were largely buffered from Mongol impact. This meant that Africa was not disrupted as some parts of the world were by the Mongol experience, but it also meant the Africans had no particular stimulus to learn from new technological opportunities. This was a null case, in other words, that would contrast quite interestingly with the experience of Western Europe.

The decline of the Mongol system could have overwhelmed the pattern of intensifying interregional contacts that we have so vigorously emphasized for the postclassical period. It certainly diverted contact opportunities. Overland contacts had to recede. The great travelers that we mentioned a session ago—the people such as Ibn Battuta, who utilized Mongol systems, as well as Islamic systems to travel such long distances in relative security—these travelers were, increasingly, a thing of the past. You couldn't do that safely over land anymore. But the system was so successful in its larger sense, the importance of exchanging goods and information was so considerable, that it readily survived the Mongols. The question, as ultimately posed by the end of the 14th century, was not whether world contacts would recede. That could have been a question; it turned out not to be because the importance of contacts was so well established. The question, rather, was: What system, under whose sponsorship, would replace the Mongols, and what routes would they use? The answer was almost surely increasing the use, once again, of waterways—but what routes would they use and what societies would particularly benefit?

This was, again, an extraordinary world history period. The last fling of the postclassical era, the system that briefly replaced the system that the Arabs had created earlier on that extended it and extended its benefits. But it was not the last gasp of global interconnections. That chapter was about to reopen in new ways in the 15th century.

.

Lecture Seventeen
Civilizations in the Americas and in Africa

Scope:

Important developments occurred in the Americas and Africa during the postclassical period, and of course, they abundantly illustrate the theme of the expanding geography of civilization as a form of human organization. The Americas offer a particular challenge because of the lack of connection to the rest of the world. One scholar, annoyed at the problems world historians have with pre-Columbian America, has written a book called *1491: Revelations of America before Columbus*. The facts remain, however, that vital American developments do not cleanly fit the larger patterns of the period and that, because of later devastation, the heritage of the Americas for subsequent history was limited as well. Africa is a different case, complicated mainly by a long tradition of historical neglect. African kingdoms and trading patterns in the postclassical period were deeply connected to the larger world network of the time. Differences from the Americas are thus clear; the really interesting comparisons involve such places as Western Europe.

Outline

I. One of the remaining puzzle pieces to fit together for the postclassical period involves the civilizations in the Americas and sub-Saharan Africa. In this lecture, we will talk about how we can use these two cases to illustrate some of the key themes of the postclassical period.

II. Civilizations in the Americas began before the postclassical period. Because the Americas were not directly connected to Asia, Europe, or Africa, the periodization of the postclassical period is somewhat artificially imposed on the Americas.

    A. Early civilizations emerged in Central America, and suggestions of early civilization are found a bit later in the Andes. The postclassical period itself captures the final flowering of Mayan civilization in Central America, the later decline of the Mayans, and the emergence of a mixed Mayan-Toltec society in parts of Central America.

B. Also in Central America, the Aztec Empire arose in the mid-14th century.

   1. The Aztecs were immigrants from the north into central Mexico and other parts of Central America.

   2. The Aztec empire would flourish during much of the 15th century.

C. The postclassical period captures the development of further civilization activities in the Andes, particularly the emergence of the Inca Empire from about 1400 onward—stretching over a long swathe of territory along the Pacific Coast of what is now Latin America.

III. Developments in American civilizations in the postclassical period emphasized continued improvements in agriculture.

   A. American societies were based on the cultivation of several key crops, including corn and potatoes. The emphasis on agriculture and the careful organization of cultivation produced amazing population concentrations and impressive cities by the 14th and 15th centuries.

   B. Trading activities were also extensive, with networks running throughout Central America.

   C. Interesting cultural forms arose in the American civilizations, seen in artistic representations of fierce gods and goddesses, as well as impressive scientific developments.

   D. The postclassical period saw a territorial expansion of American civilizations and a flowering of cultural and economic developments.

IV. Scholars debate the question of how to place American patterns into a larger world framework in this pre-Columbian, postclassical age.

   A. Charles Mann recently published *1491: Revelations of the Americas before Columbus*, in which he takes world historians to task for failing to do full justice to the richness and detail of pre-1492 American history.

B. These societies had no effective contact with other parts of the world. Although this isolation did not hamper their development before or during the postclassical period, it did create vulnerabilities once contact was established.

C. American societies lacked certain technologies, such as the use of metal for weaponry or tools and the use of wheels on devices other than toys.

D. The Americas lacked a rich mix of animals that were candidates for domestication.

E. Because they had no routine contact with other parts of the world, peoples in the Americas were vulnerable to diseases that had been acclimatized in Afro-Eurasia, notably, smallpox and the measles. Once contact was established, American societies would suffer dreadfully.

F. The divide between the Americas before contact and the Americas after contact is crucial; given the vulnerabilities in the Americas in technology, animal domestication, and disease immunity, developments there would be superseded by European and African patterns.

G. The Americas may have had occasional contacts from other civilizations, but these contacts were not sufficient to counteract this region's isolation from the world network.

V. The Americas offer some comparisons with other early civilizations.

A. Some scholars have noted a vague similarity between the Inca Empire, with its emphasis on a divine ruler, and ancient Egypt. This can be contrasted with a slightly more Mesopotamian civilization, such as Central America.

B. Although American society was overwhelmed after 1492, it was not obliterated. Important traces of earlier artistic impulses, polytheistic religion, and aspects of local village organization and agricultural practices would survive, particularly in Central America and the Andes.

C. It is important to recognize that the legacy here was limited. The problem of integrating the American patterns of the postclassical period with larger patterns remains considerable.

VI. In contrast to the Americas, Africa fits quite well into the larger patterns of the postclassical period, including its involvement with the world network.

  A. Agriculture and ironworking were introduced early in Africa, and the spread of these developments south of the Sahara proceeded relatively steadily before and during the postclassical period.

  1. In a process known as the *great Bantu migrations*, peoples originally located in west-central Africa moved southward and eastward, bringing with them agriculture, ironworking, and new kinds of political organization.

  2. The spread of the Bantus was a major development in terms of connections among African language groups.

  B. Early civilization activities in sub-Saharan Africa focused in the upper Nile area in some connection to developments in Egypt.

  1. Significant states and cultures developed in Kush and Aksum, followed by the establishment of an Ethiopian state.

  2. These activities took place in connection with patterns in the Middle East and the eastern Mediterranean, which is one reason that Ethiopia received early influences from Judaism and Christianity.

  C. In the postclassical period itself, two centers of activity developed in Africa.

  1. The Swahili Belt stretched along the Indian Ocean coast in mixed Arab-African communities. This region encompassed an active set of trading societies and developed a written language and political organizations of the city-state type.

  2. Larger kingdoms featuring powerful rulers emerged in sub-Saharan West Africa. Sometimes called *Sudanic* after the Arab word for "black," these kingdoms experienced increasing trade activity, including activity that would connect West Africa across the Sahara to North Africa and the Middle East.

VII. In fitting sub-Saharan African patterns into the larger network of world history, we need to explore a few issues.

   A. It is possible to suggest a few characteristic African themes, particularly in the Sudanic kingdoms of West Africa.

      1. These civilizations were vigorously polytheistic and used polytheism to emphasize the close connections between human activities and the forces and features of nature.

      2. These civilizations tended to emphasize the divinity of major rulers.

      3. These civilizations focused on extended families and the connections between individuals in this life and ancestors.

      4. These fairly general features can be used to provide at least some baseline for discussions of African characteristics that cut across states and even larger regions.

   B. There is a complicated relationship between African developments before and during the postclassical period and the great religious and philosophical systems that developed elsewhere.

      1. African development featured the manipulation of great traditions, particularly those derived from Islam and Christianity.

      2. In both the Sudanic kingdoms and the Swahili Belt, African developments were powerfully influenced by Islam. Outside the Swahili Belt, however, Islam did not, at this early point, become a mass religion.

VIII. Sub-Saharan African history in the postclassical period should be viewed in much the same framework that we used for Japan, Russia, Southeast Asia, and Western Europe.

   A. Sub-Saharan Africa is another civilization in active contact with the most prosperous centers of the world, benefiting from trade with these centers and imitating some of their features but also maintaining a separate sphere of existence.

B. One African historian has proposed a close comparison between developments in sub-Saharan Africa during the postclassical period and those in Western Europe. Using a rough date of 1250 CE, he argues that the similarities in these societies are quite striking.

    1. Both civilizations contained significant kingdoms, larger in Africa and loosely organized. Although Africa did not develop literal feudalism, its rule had some overtones of the jockeying necessary in European feudal monarchies.

    2. Both civilizations developed new commercial centers and saw increased activity linking commerce to the Mediterranean and Middle East.

    3. In both civilizations merchant activities were important not only in their own right but also in stimulating other economic developments and political activity.

C. If one looks at the same two societies 200 years later, however, the comparative situation changes markedly.

    1. European societies, particularly Spain and Portugal, were actively engaged in exploratory trips down the African coast and were experiencing rapid changes in political and cultural systems.

    2. African kingdoms did not exhibit the same kind of outreach and commitment to major change as Western Europe, largely because they did not face the same need for outreach as Western Europe.

D. The year 1450 finds the fates of these two societies beginning to diverge.

Further Reading:

Robert Sharer, *The Ancient Maya.*

Michael Moseley, *The Incas and Their Ancestors: The Archeology of Peru.*

Philip Curtin, et al., *African History from Earliest Times to Independence,* 2nd ed.

Charles C. Mann, *1491: New Revelations of the Americas before Columbus.*

Questions to Consider:

1. How important is pre-Columbian American history in world history? What's the best case for relatively substantial attention?

2. If West Africa compares favorably with Western Europe around 1250, in terms of international role, trade, and even politics, how and why does the comparison around 1450 begin to look so different?

Lecture Seventeen—Transcript
Civilizations in the Americas and in Africa

One of the remaining puzzle pieces to fit together for the postclassical period involves dealing with civilizations in the Americas and sub-Saharan Africa. Pretty obviously, that's the focus of our discussion right now. Both cases illustrate the broad theme of the expansion of the geographical range and variety of civilizations in the postclassical period, but we need to do more than simply mention that obvious fact. We need to talk about how we can use these final two cases directly or, in one case, indirectly to illustrate some of the other key themes of the postclassical period.

Civilizations in the Americas began before the postclassical period. Indeed, for fairly obvious reasons, since the Americas were not directly connected to Asia, Europe, and Africa, the periodization of the postclassical period is somewhat artificially imposed on the Americas. Early civilizations emerged in Central America and suggestions of early civilization also a bit later in the Andes. The postclassical period itself captures the final flowering of Mayan civilization in Central America, the later decline of the Mayans, and the emergence of a mixed Mayan-Toltec society in many parts of Central America. Then, finally, still in Central America, was the emergence in the mid-14th century of a new Aztec Empire. The Aztecs were in-migrants from the north coming into central Mexico and other parts of Central America. This Aztec Empire was constructed in the later 14th century and would flourish during much of the 15th. The postclassical period also captures the development of further civilization activities in the Andes—particularly, though quite late in the postclassical period, the emergence of the Inca Empire from about 1400 onward, stretching over an amazingly long swathe of territory along the Pacific Coast of what is now Latin America.

Key developments in American civilizations in this postclassical period obviously emphasized the continued improvements in agriculture. American societies were based on the cultivation of several key crops, particularly corn, but also in the Andes, the potato. A number of other additional crops were added to this mix. The emphasis on agriculture, the careful organization of cultivation, produced some amazing population concentrations and opportunities for the emergence of impressive cities by the 14th and 15th centuries. Probably as many as 25 million people concentrated in the central

Mexican plateau around the capital city of the Aztecs. This was a concentration that rivaled any other in the world. It would greatly impress early European visitors, who marveled at the monumental style of buildings in the cities; again, the careful organization of agriculture around irrigation systems, carefully terraced hillsides, etc. Agriculture and a carefully organized agricultural economy was one key feature of these American civilizations. Trading activities were also extensive. Trading networks ran through Central America. The Inca Empire was based on trading patterns that actually not just connected different parts of the Inca territory but ran up and down the Andes Mountains, with different specializations at each level and trade along this altitude parameter, as well.

Along with economy, agriculture, and trade, a second focus for the American civilizations involves the emergence of impressive and interesting cultural forms. These were polytheistic societies often, particularly in Central America, focusing on some rather fierce gods and goddesses, some of whom took animal form, which would inspire some interesting and dramatic art. American culture, particularly again in Central America, also emphasized impressive scientific developments. The Mayans were one of only a few societies independently to develop the concept of zero. They introduced an elaborate set of calendar calculations, among other things. They were aware that the Earth is round. The scientific achievements of this society were most impressive, indeed.

The postclassical period sees an expansion territorially of American civilizations and a further flowering of cultural and economic developments. Two impressive empires develop toward the end of the postclassical period, both of them, both the Aztec and the Inca, based on tributes paid by subject people. In the case of Central America, particularly, there was extensive use of slavery, but this is a key set of societies that needs to be added to the list of crucial developments in the postclassical period.

This said, there is a question, and it has been fairly vigorously debated, about how you place the American patterns into a larger world framework in this pre-Columbian, postclassical age. Charles Mann recently published a very impressive book, a big book, called *1491*, in which he takes world historians, including myself in one of my textbooks, to task by name for failing to do full justice to the richness and detail of pre-1492 American history. The point is well taken, but there are a couple of issues that I would continue to stress even in acknowledging the impressive historical work that increasingly builds our picture of what American societies were like and how rich and varied they were before the arrival of the Europeans.

The key point from a world history standpoint, in addition to registering all these important cases and indicating some of their main outlines, is to recognize that these societies were indeed isolated. They had no effective contact with other parts of the world. While this in no sense hampered their development during the postclassical period or, indeed, before—again, impressive economic achievements, impressive monuments, impressive cultural apparatus—it did create certain vulnerabilities once contact was established, which obviously began in 1492.

The vulnerabilities were these: First of all, American societies, for all their impressive economic achievements—and in many ways this fact makes the achievements even more significant—lacked certain key technologies. They had no metal use. They used gold and silver for ornamentation, but their weaponry, their tools did not embrace metals. Obviously, had they had contact with other societies where metal use was established, this would have been fairly automatic. Nor did they utilize the wheel. They had wheels on toys, interestingly, but they did not incorporate wheels into other aspects of their activities. Again, this can make their capacity to build large, dense population networks all the more impressive, but it certainly made them vulnerable comparatively once contact was established. A technology gap is a key point. An animal gap is a second point. The Americas possessed relatively few domesticated animals. There were guinea pigs, there were dogs, and there were turkeys— obviously, potential sources of food, all. In the Andes, there were light-burden-carrying animals in the llamas and alpacas, but the rich mix of potentially domesticable animals that existed in Afro-Eurasia was simply absent in the Americas. This also would be a liability, not before 1492, but once contact was established. Most important, of course, was a disease gap. Because they had no routine contact with other parts of the world, peoples in the Americas were extraordinarily vulnerable to diseases that had been acclimatized in Afro-Eurasia—notably, diseases such as smallpox and the measles. Again, it didn't matter during the postclassical period; there was no new exposure. But once contact was established, again, American societies would suffer and, frankly, suffer quite dreadfully.

This means, obviously, that the 1492 divide between the Americas before contact and the Americas after contact is particularly crucial, because given technology, animal, and disease vulnerabilities, American developments would be more fully superseded by European and African patterns. American political, social, and cultural leadership would, in essence, be decapitated. That means, in turn, there's less obvious continuity between the Americas in the postclassical period and what would happen next. It's very important to recognize that the developments in the Americas were significant. It's important, also, to discuss possibilities of casual contact—I have students all the time who come up with the knowledge of this or that National Geographic special and say, "But didn't the Polynesians have an expedition that drifted to the Americas? Wasn't there contact with Asia?" The answer is, frankly, maybe yes, but it didn't matter. That is because no contact was established that was significant enough to remove the Americas from this category of isolation from the larger world network. Significant contact, obviously, would have brought technological diffusion, would have brought animal diffusion, and would have brought disease diffusion. That would have altered the face of American history well before 1492.

There are reasons to study the Americas. They can usefully be compared with other early civilizations. Some scholars have noted a vague similarity, for example, between the Inca Empire, with its emphasis on a divine ruler, and ancient Egypt. They've contrasted this with a slightly more Mesopotamian-like Central America. This kind of comparison is a useful addition to our analysis of early civilizations, although it may not do full justice to the Americas. There were certainly American legacies to the wider world, particularly in the category of food, and we don't want to forget these aspects either. Finally, perhaps most important, although American society was overwhelmed after 1492, it was not absolutely obliterated. Important traces of earlier artistic impulses, important traces of polytheistic religion that could be fused with Catholic saints, for example, and important aspects of local village organization and agricultural practices—these would survive, particularly in areas such as Central America and the Andes, where concentrations of Native American populations were particularly great. But it's also important to recognize that the legacy here was limited. The problem of figuring out how to integrate the American patterns of the postclassical period with the larger patterns remains considerable. I should add very briefly that something of a similar dilemma applies to activities in Pacific Oceania during the postclassical period. Here, too, societies had developed early and they then became isolated from larger patterns. Important activities occurred in, for example, Polynesia during the postclassical period, with the establishment of human settlements in what is now known as New Zealand. But, again, these patterns, which were somewhat less elaborate than the civilizations of the Americas—though they included interesting artistic efforts and interesting social and political structures—these efforts also have to be taken as a separate case, an isolated case that merely has to be noted. It can't easily be fit into the larger patterns of world history during this period.

The case of sub-Saharan Africa is absolutely different and, indeed, there's a risk in pairing Africa and the Americas in this period. The clearest connection is a fallacious one, but it needs to be mentioned. Until fairly recently, African history was viewed as almost as much a no man's land as American history has been viewed until recently. Example: I had the privilege a decade or so ago of working on an encyclopedia of world history, a new edition. The earlier edition, which was extremely impressive and involved all sorts of significant scholarship, devoted literally one page to developments in sub-Saharan Africa from the origins of social activity until the end of the postclassical period, i.e., until the arrival of the Europeans. While this coverage had a few interesting bits of data, it was shrouded with statements such as how early African history is covered by obscurity, etc., etc., etc. This is absolutely wrong. We now know a lot about postclassical African history and even African history before that point. We know that it was quite varied and we know that, in fact, in contrast to the Americas, it fit quite directly into the larger patterns of the postclassical period, including active connections with what we've described earlier as the world network.

Agriculture and ironworking were introduced early into Africa and, in the case of agriculture, may have actually been independently invented there. We can't be sure. Again, we know there were several cases of discrete invention and the African case is a possibility. The spread of agriculture and ironwork south of the Sahara proceeded relatively steadily before the postclassical period and then during the early centuries of the postclassical period. An important effort of diffusion was undertaken in a process known as the *great Bantu migrations*, with peoples originally located in west-central Africa steadily migrating southward and then eastward, bringing agriculture and ironworking with them and, in their wake, increasingly also possibilities for new kinds of political organization. The spread of the Bantus was a major development also in terms of connections among African language groups. It's an important process, which again precedes the postclassical period, but continues during its early phases, as well.

Early civilized activities in sub-Saharan Africa focused, as we've already noted, in the upper Nile area, in some connection to the developments in Egypt. Significant states and cultures developed in Kush and Aksum in the upper Nile region. Then, there followed the development of Ethiopia and the establishment of an Ethiopian state. These activities were in considerable connection with patterns in the Middle East and the eastern Mediterranean, which is one reason that Ethiopia very early received influences from Judaism and then, later, from Christianity, becoming one of the major Christian strongholds on the sub-Saharan African subcontinent.

In the postclassical period, as we have already suggested in early discussions, two centers of activity developed, particularly in sub-Saharan Africa. One stretched along the Indian Ocean coast in mixed Arab-African communities—the Swahili Belt—a very active set of trading societies, developing a written language and city-state type political organizations, obviously in close commercial and cultural contact with the Middle East, particularly.

Larger kingdoms emerged in sub-Saharan West Africa. Sometimes they're called Sudanic kingdoms after the Arab word for "black." They began with the kingdom of Ghana, which actually originated slightly before the postclassical period. These kingdoms—and there were numerous examples—featured, frequently, fairly large territorial holdings, powerful rulers, kings who could claim great authority and who would surround themselves with impressive rituals and considerable majesty. The territories also experienced increasing trade activity, including trade activity that would connect West Africa across the Sahara to North Africa and the Middle East. The capacity to tax merchant activities was one of the sources of revenue of these newly imposing states. Cultural apparatus proceeded considerably, as well. West African art featured a variety of designs but a fairly close emphasis on work in sculpture in both metalworking and woodworking, creating designs that continue to have a characteristic resonance when you look at African artistic patterns in a larger global context. In other words, this was a period of important commercial, political, and cultural development in West Africa.

There are a couple of interesting questions that need to be addressed in characterizing the sub-Saharan African patterns, again, in a framework that can be fit into the larger network of world history. The first question is the most fundamental. This is a great big place. The African subcontinent is the second largest landmass in the world, second only to Asia. It has all sorts of climatic conditions, all sorts of geographical features, and it is forcing things a bit to talk about African civilization when so much variety exists. Still, while recognizing this issue, it is possible to suggest that there were a few characteristic African themes that would crop up, particularly in the Sudanic kingdoms of West Africa, but in some cases beyond, as well.

Theme number one was a vigorous emphasis on polytheism and a use of polytheism to emphasize the close connections between human activities and the forces and features of nature. This is not necessarily a strikingly different version of polytheism, but it certainly provided a cultural explanation for a variety of phenomena for Africans. It served as the framework for a good bit of natural medicine, a combination of herbal treatments and invocations of divine spirits. It was an important cultural framework. The second feature—again, particularly vivid in West Africa—was a tendency to emphasize the divinity of major rulers. Divine kingship, not a uniquely African product, was an important feature of many African political efforts. Emphasis on extended families and the connections between individuals in this life and ancestors was a third feature. African families frequently, for example, banded together to protect widows. It was not uncommon in many regions of Africa for families to feel an obligation for a brother of a deceased husband to marry a widow, and there can be emphasis here on the importance of social solidarity, the importance of familial protection. These features, fairly general, I admit, can be used to give at least some baseline for discussions of African characteristics that would cut across particular states and even larger regions.

A second question about Africa, which goes back to the long uncertainty about African history before the arrival of Europeans, is the complicated relationship between African developments in the postclassical period and before and what we might call the great traditions, the great religious and philosophical systems that, frankly, for the most part, developed elsewhere and not in sub-Saharan Africa proper. Sub-Saharan Africa was a recipient of great traditions, just as, frankly, Europe had been. We need to recognize that African development would feature the manipulation of great traditions and the combination of these traditions with more local elements. Africans did not collectively seize, in the long run, on only one tradition; they utilized several, particularly traditions derived both from Islam and from Christianity. There's simply a feature here that needs to be recognized. It doesn't detract from the variety and importance of developments in sub-Saharan Africa during the postclassical period. The notion that this is simply a vast, mysterious, and frankly backwards society is an absolute myth that reflects racial assumptions and prejudices on the part of Western scholars until quite recently. Throw that away. There still are some distinctive features and they can be recognized.

A particular twist on this that we've touched on already, obviously, was the fairly complicated relationship between postclassical sub-Saharan Africa and the forces of Islam. Both in the Sudanic kingdoms and in the Swahili Belt, African developments were directly connected with Islam and powerfully influenced by Islam. But particularly in the Sudanic kingdoms, particularly in West Africa, Islam was taken in a somewhat distinctive way. African rulers welcomed Islamic merchants, and obviously, Islam helped bridge connections between commercial activities below the Sahara and the larger trading patterns of North Africa and the Middle East. African rulers also welcomed Muslims as scholars and officials. Islam provided literate bureaucrats. Islam provided people who had experience in other bureaucratic systems. There was a strong Islamic cast to the African kingdoms, particularly from the midpoint of the development of Ghana onward. It featured commercial connections. It featured some occasional military contacts and raids. It definitely featured a strong cultural interest. From the great kingdom of Mali would emerge the scholarly city of Timbuktu, one of the real centers of Islamic learning during the later postclassical period, a center that easily compares with some of the intellectual centers developed in

Western Europe during the same period. But outside the Swahili Belt, Islam did not, at this early point, become a mass religion in sub-Saharan Africa. Most Africans remained polytheistic, and this was simply a distinctive African combination. It just has to be taken as the way this connection with Islam developed. Muslim travelers—and we've noted this already with Ibn Battuta—would also note that even some African Muslims, while they were pious, while they followed the injunctions of the Koran faithfully, including going on pilgrimages to Mecca—the pilgrimage of one great African king, Mansa Musa, was a tremendous splash because he brought so much gold with him that he briefly dislocated the banking systems in places such as Egypt—but many African Muslims did not practice Islam exactly the same way as it was practiced in North Africa and the Middle East, particularly gender aspects. The freedoms and public opportunities allowed to women were not exactly subsumed into the Middle Eastern-North African version of Islam. Again, it's a distinctive amalgamation, while recognizing the importance of the overall connections to the Islamic world.

Basically, the most important point is to see that sub-Saharan African history in the postclassical period needs to be treated in much the same framework that we used for Japan, Russia, Southeast Asia, and Western Europe. Sub-Saharan Africa was another case of a civilization in active contact with the most prosperous centers of the world, benefiting from trade with these centers and imitating, at least to some degree—as in the utilization of Islam for purposes of scholarship and political activities—but also maintaining a certain separate sphere of existence. In this vein, one African historian has proposed a particularly close comparison between developments in sub-Saharan Africa during the postclassical period and those in Western Europe. He seizes on a rough date of 1250 and argues that if you look at sub-Saharan Africa and Western Europe in 1250 CE, in broad outline, the similarities are actually quite striking. In both cases, there were significant kingdoms; they tended to be larger in Africa than in Europe but more loosely organized. African kings might claim divine kingship, but in fact, their power rested on careful negotiation and conciliation of the warrior class. While Africa did not develop literal feudalism, this had some overtones of the jockeying necessary in the European feudal monarchies. Both Africa and Europe were developing new commercial centers. Merchant classes were on the rise. Both saw increased activity linking commercial patterns to those of the Mediterranean and the Middle East. And, again, in both instances, merchant activities were important not only in their own right but in stimulating other economic developments—for example, mining in the case of Africa—and in stimulating political activity, as well, as we have seen. These, then, were cases in which you had two emerging civilization areas, still fairly loosely structured politically, though with definite states and political apparatus, exploring commercial opportunities, exploring new cultural expressions, etc.

The same comparison, however—and this is the point on which we'll end—also notes that if you take the two societies 200 years later, in 1450, the comparative situation changes markedly. By 1450—and we'll explore this a little more fully next time—European societies, particularly Spain and Portugal, were actively engaged in exploratory trips down the African coast. They were reaching out toward new world roles. They were developing more rapid changes in political and cultural systems. African societies, in no sense, were lagging compared to their own past. Kingdoms ebbed and flowed; the kingdom of Ghana had yielded to the rise of Mali. By the end of the postclassical period, Mali is fading somewhat and will be placed by another network of kingdoms, including the Songhai dynasty. These were ebbs and flows that really didn't distort the basic framework of African history, but there is not the same kind of outreach and commitment to major change. The final question is: Why? The answer involves several factors that shed light back on postclassical African history, as well.

Factor number one was sheer geography. Western Europe possesses an abundant river system that creates navigable possibilities connecting inland areas to the oceans. Sub-Saharan Africa, for the most part, does not. African rivers are not easily navigable from the ocean inland, and they were, therefore, less obvious as a stimulus for seagoing activities. Except for the Swahili coast, Africans did not develop a significant commitment to naval activities during the postclassical period or, obviously, before. There was geography. Second was the relationship to Islam. For Western Europe, trading with Islam was always tense. It was always, to some degree, trading with the enemy. There was always a certain level of resentment and anxiety. For Africans, trading with Islam was non-problematic; it was fine. Africans were either Muslims or familiar with Muslims.

They didn't have a problem here to be solved. Third was balance of payments. Western Europe, as we've noted previously, had significant difficulty in coming up with goods that they could use in exchange for products they wanted from world trade. Africa had much less of an issue here. They traded slaves, they traded gold, and they traded other agricultural products. I don't mean there was never an economic issue, but there was not the same kind of problem to be solved as existed in Western Europe. Finally—as we've also noted before—Africa, unlike Europe, had had no particular interaction with the Mongol interlude and, therefore, no particular opportunity to connect to new sources of technological change. Again, this was a contrast with Europe.

The year 1450 finds the fates of these two societies beginning to diverge; in a way, reflecting how successful postclassical African developments had been. Africa did not face the same need for difficult transitions, for ambitious outreach that Western Europe did. Perhaps this was unfortunate, but it was at the very least an ironic cap to a very important and impressive period in the history of sub-Saharan African societies.

Lecture Eighteen
The World in 1450

Scope:

A number of crucial changes took place by the middle of the 15th century, many of which would set the stage for the next period in world history. Several of the developments were conditioned by the decline of the Arabs and the receding of the Mongol empires. The most familiar, undeniably important change involved the increasing explorations by Europeans down the African coast; this pattern, however, must be put into a world historical perspective. China made a number of crucial decisions in this period also, extending and then ending a fascinating series of expeditions. Russia, by 1450, was casting off Mongol rule but was also deeply affected by the death throes of the Byzantine Empire. Change in the Middle East highlighted the rise of the Ottoman Turks, a development with implications for Europe and Russia as well. Quite coincidentally, changes in the Americas prepared for later shifts in the global mix.

Outline

I. Almost all world historians agree that around 1450 or 1500 a significant break occurred in world history.

   A. By 1450, the great era of Arab politics and merchant activity had passed, as had the Mongol era.

   B. Given the demise of these two great systems and the continued importance of interregional economic and cultural contacts, what kind of system would replace these previous frameworks?

II. Specific developments in the first half of the 15th century focused on China.

   A. With the expulsion of the Mongols from China at the end of the 14th century, the Ming dynasty came to power. Like many new dynasties, it was vigorous, benefiting from an expanding economy and interested in new political statements and a degree of territorial expansion.

B. Beginning in 1405, under the Ming, the Chinese mounted a series of huge expeditions that took troops, goods, and political and cultural representatives from the Pacific Coast of China through Southeast Asia to East Asia, South Asia, West Asia, and the Indian Ocean coast of Africa.

    1. These expeditions were likely mounted to extend the Chinese custom of seeking tribute from neighboring contacts.

    2. For 30 years, these expeditions provided the most striking interregional contacts operating during the 15th century as a whole.

    3. The expeditions were successful in bringing Chinese connections to Indonesia and other parts of Southeast Asia; in establishing a new Chinese presence in India; and in establishing links directly with the Middle East, particularly the Persian Gulf region, and with the states of East Africa.

    4. The expeditions were an important assertion of economic strength, building on the established position of Chinese manufacturing that had begun in the Song dynasty and had been extended under the Mongol Yuan dynasty.

C. In 1433, the expeditions were ended by imperial decision.

    1. There may have been a certain traditionalist bureaucratic suspicion of these costly expeditions on the grounds that they overemphasized naval activities and commercial groups.

    2. A new Ming emperor wanted to establish policies that would be different from those of his predecessor.

    3. It is also possible that although the expeditions had resulted in considerable tribute, the crude economic calculation—in terms of short-run cost benefits—argued for termination.

D. The new representative of the dynasty further believed that investment monies should go to two other important projects.

    1. One project was a new Ming capital in Beijing.

    2. Another project was the reconstruction of the Great Wall of China (to keep the Mongols at bay).

E. The end of the Chinese expeditions did not end China's economic role in world trade, nor did it isolate China from the rest of the world. It did, however, signal an end to the brief flurry of Chinese initiative into the rest of the world.

III. A second center of developments around 1450 involved the Middle East and southeast Europe.

   A. The decline of Arab rule in these regions left openings for the immigration of new peoples from Central Asia, particularly the Osmanli Turks or Ottoman Turks, who began to appear around 1450.

   B. The Ottoman Turks were fervent Muslims, heavily influenced by Sufism. As they migrated into the area, they seized territories from Arab states and focused on attacking the Byzantine Empire.

      1. A major player during the postclassical period, the Byzantine Empire had been declining for some decades before 1450; this decline made the empire a prime target for this new series of interlopers.

      2. The Turks laid siege to Constantinople, and in 1453 the city fell and was renamed Istanbul; this fall is one of the great events in world history.

      3. For the Middle East, the fall represented a clear step in the establishment of the Ottoman Empire, which would provide a new source of political and military power to a region that had been fragmented for almost two centuries.

   C. The fall of Constantinople also represented a new opportunity for the Turks and Islam to move into the Balkans and southeastern Europe.

      1. Even before the fall, the Turks had seized territories in parts of modern-day Greece; thus the change for southeastern Europe was in many ways just as great as the impending change for parts of the Middle East.

      2. The Byzantine Empire had been the model for Russian development, and the collapse of Constantinople represented both a terrifying challenge to the Russian sense of identity and gave Russia a new sense of itself as heir to the mission of the old empire.

D. The fall of Constantinople was a symbolic and real challenge to other parts of Europe, including Western Europe.

    1. West Europeans, particularly Italians, had treated Constantinople scornfully in the last days of the Byzantine Empire.

    2. West Europeans ignored appeals from later Byzantine emperors for assistance against the assailing Turks, but when the city fell, Europeans had to face the fact that a bastion of Christianity had been removed in favor of a new and fairly potent Islamic presence.

E. In conjunction with these developments, Russian political rulers began to fully cast off Mongol rule in the early-15th century. By 1450, a steadily expansionist Russian state was forming around Moscow, and the fall of Byzantium served as an additional spur.

IV. Not every place in the world changed or changed significantly in 1450.

A. Africa experienced basic continuity, despite political shifts and changes in trading patterns. The rise of the kingdom of Songhai was an important development in the Sudanic region.

B. 1450 was not a striking point in Japanese development even though some adjustment took place.

C. Developments in India were not marked by any dramatic shifts around 1450. The more dramatic changes would come 50 or 70 years later with a new series of Islamic invasions into India.

V. We also find significant developments in the Americas.

A. By 1450, both the Aztecs and the Incas were beginning to encounter new challenges to their rule.

B. Quite independent of other events, then, the political structures of the late postclassical period in the Americas were beginning to unravel. This would facilitate European entry after 1492.

VI. The final series of developments occurred in new forms of European outreach.

    A. Beginning as early as the 13th century, individual merchants and rulers had shown some interest in breaking the confines of European geography and its focus on the Mediterranean as an artery of trade.

    B. Farther to the north, Scandinavians had crossed the Atlantic and reached North America, then retreated to more interesting and durable settlements in Greenland and Iceland.

    C. By the early-15th century, patterns of exploration down the African coast were extended. This exploration was sponsored by the king of Portugal, newly freed from Muslim control, and by rulers in Spain.

        1. The explorations pushed steadily down the African coast, partly in search of gold.

        2. The larger framework, however, was the recognition that Europe faced difficulties in postclassical interregional relationships.

        3. The Europeans had developed a taste for Asian goods but not the capacity to pay for these goods; by seeking new sources of gold and other opportunities, the Europeans were trying to remedy a clear problem in their interregional outreach.

        4. Europeans also wondered if they could find a direct connection with Asia around the African coast to avoid Islamic middlemen and cultural challenges.

        5. This interest in finding solutions to the cultural and economic problems of dependence on Islamic merchants was further galvanized by the fall of Constantinople and the new potential for Muslim organization in the eastern Mediterranean.

VII. The conventional textbooks on West European history offer a somewhat different background to these new expeditions.

A. By 1450, European political capacity was beginning to improve. The feudal monarchies in England, France, and increasingly Spain and Portugal had achieved a bit more central control over their territories. They also had somewhat greater capacity to guide trade policy and mount significant exploratory expeditions.

B. European Christianity, not a new force, may have been given a new lease on life in terms of missionary spirit by the expulsion of the Muslims from the Iberian Peninsula. Spanish and, to a lesser degree, Portuguese Catholic leaders played prominent roles in the explorations that began to take shape in the 15th century.

C. We also need to acknowledge new attitudes developing in the Renaissance, first in Italy and, by 1450, spreading more widely. The Renaissance brought new attention to this-worldly activities and suggested new confidence in the potential of individual achievement.

D. Nonetheless, the world history picture continues to be more complicated than a focus on just the West allows. Key problems remained in terms of world position, including the issue of Islamic intermediaries and the need to compensate for Islamic control in the eastern Mediterranean.

VIII. As the expeditions unfolded in 1450 and afterward, they reveal a few other points that bring us back to motivations.

A. The expeditions failed to find massive troves of new wealth, although they did find some new territories. Europeans began to take over island groups in the southern Atlantic, such as the Azores and the Canaries.

B. The native populations of these islands were extremely vulnerable to some of the common diseases brought by the Europeans, resulting in rapid depopulation. This was, at once, a useful development for the Europeans—local resistance was minimal—and a challenge because of the obvious need to find additional sources of labor.

C. The solution adopted was to raid the northwest African mainland, where slavery was well established, for sources of labor. The Europeans began to import African slaves into these island groups with the purpose of establishing sugar cultivation.

D. This policy was perfectly understandable in terms of European interest: The Europeans had an economic problem, and growing sugar—rather than importing it from Asia—was at least a partial remedy. Nonetheless, this policy of economic exploitation raised some interesting questions about the nature of the European role in the world as Europeans gained new levels of power.

E. Once the Europeans succeeded in rounding the southern tip of Africa and reaching Asia directly, they still had a balance-of-payments problem.

    1. When Vasco da Gama returned to India for a second time after 1500, he brought a solution to this problem in the form of guns.

    2. Da Gama deliberately slaughtered a number of Indian officials to induce the rest of the population to trade, even though the Europeans did not yet have much to offer in the exchange.

IX. Moving forward from 1450, a variety of developments occurred in a number of different places.

A. Both the Chinese expeditions and their curtailment set the stage for European initiatives that would form a new framework for interregional trade.

B. Developments in the Middle East, the arrival of the Turks, the fall of one of the great Christian empires, and the beginning of new assertions by Russians also need to be factored into the world picture.

C. The end of the postclassical period saw the gradual emergence of a new system of interregional trade that would be immensely important, but it also saw power and cultural shifts in other regions. It also set the stage for a complex pattern of development in world history's next period.

Further Reading:

Kenneth Pomeranz, *The Great Divergence: China, Europe, and the Making of the Modern World Economy.*

David Northrup, *Africa's Discovery of Europe, 1450–1850.*

Felipe Fernandez-Armesto, *Millennium.*

Questions to Consider:

1. Should China have continued its overseas expeditions, and how much difference would this have made in world history later on?

2. How much should the standard explanations of the "rise of the West" beginning in the 15th century be modified in light of Europe's problems and the ongoing strengths of other societies? Where does the European Renaissance fit in the larger panorama of world history?

Lecture Eighteen—Transcript
The World in 1450

Almost all world historians agree that 1450 or 1500 constitutes a significant break in world history. Today, we're going to talk about developments in 1450. We'll make a brief bow at the end to 1500. I don't think the tensions here are terribly significant. We're going to be talking about 1450 in terms of significant changes taking shape in a number of different regions of the world, not just one. The context, just by way of reminder, is twofold. First of all, by 1450, the great era of Arab politics and merchant activity has passed. Arabs are still a vigorous people; there are a number of Arab states; Arab religious and cultural activity remains considerable. But the central role that the caliphate and the Arab version of Islam had played is obviously over. Also over is the Mongol era, definitively by 1450. There are still pockets of Mongol rule. There are pockets of Mongol population, for example, in the Crimea, where a Tatar minority exists to this day, expelled by Stalin and newly returned since the fall of communism, but the Mongol era is over. An overarching question in the world in 1450 was, given the demise of these two great systems, which had so dominated the postclassical period and its transitional ending and given the continued importance of interregional economic and cultural contacts, what kind of system would come to be in the place of these previous frameworks?

Specific developments focused initially on China. The big news during the first half of the 15th century was actually primarily Chinese news. The Mongols had been expelled from China at the end of the 14th century. A new dynasty, the Ming, was in power in China. As with many new dynasties, it was full of vim and vigor, benefiting from an expanding economy, interested in new political statements, and interested in territorial expansion to a degree, although remember, the Chinese have never historically been devoted to expansion as a primary guiding principle.

Under the Ming, beginning in 1405, a series of Chinese expeditions were mounted, which took Chinese troops and goods and political and cultural representatives from the Pacific coast of China, through Southeast Asia, to East Asia, to South Asia, to West Asia, and to the Indian Ocean coast of Africa. These great expeditions were organized in huge ships, so large that they actually could carry not only domesticated animals but gardens to feed the expeditions as they moved along. These huge expeditions were probably mounted primarily to extend the old Chinese custom of seeking tribute from neighboring contacts. Certainly, the expeditions were actively utilized in this vein, with political representatives from several of the visited territories coming back to China bringing tribute with them, sometimes held until they provided appropriate tribute in turn. A specific goal of establishing more politics-free commercial networks was probably not involved. Be that as it may, for virtually 30 years, the Chinese expeditions, mounted every several years, provided the most striking interregional contacts that were operating during the 15th century as a whole. These expeditions were commanded, interestingly, by a Muslim Chinese, a eunuch named Cheng Ho. These expeditions were extremely successfully in bringing Chinese connections to Indonesia and other parts of Southeast Asia; in, obviously, establishing a new kind of Chinese presence in India; and in establishing new Chinese links directly with the Middle East, particularly the Persian Gulf region, and with the states of East Africa. Chinese coins and other artifacts have been found from these expeditions in considerable abundance. Speculation has one wondering, as the Chinese expeditions moved along the East African coast, at some point, did the expeditions reach the southern tip of Africa and peek into the Atlantic, and did the leaders wonder, should we go there? They didn't. We don't know that for sure.

Recently, one historian has written a book arguing that one of the Chinese expeditions actually crossed the Pacific. It's an amazing piece of historical imagination based on essentially no evidence whatsoever, and there's no reason to think it's accurate, but even dismissing this, this was an important series of expeditions, a delightful episode in world history, and an important assertion of Chinese economic strength. Remember, these expeditions built on the established position of Chinese manufacturing that had begun to be embellished in the Song dynasty, extended under the Mongol Yuan dynasty, and now obviously, confirmed by this explosion of a statement of Chinese dynamism and commercial and military strength.

But the expeditions ended in 1433 by an imperial decision. The motives for this decision seem to have been several. There may have been a certain traditionalist bureaucratic suspicion of these costly expeditions on grounds that they gave too much attention to naval activities, too much attention to commercial groups. We don't know that, and it's important not to overdo the conservatism that this decision implies. There certainly were specific factors. A new Ming emperor had come to the throne and, as many political newcomers, he wanted to establish that his policies were going to be different from those of his predecessor. Probably a certain amount of sheer whim entered in. It's also possible that while the tribute received from the expeditions had been considerable, the crude economic calculation—at least, in terms of short-run cost benefits—argued for termination.

Without question—and I think these two are the more important causal factors—the new representative of the dynasty felt that there were two more important purposes for investment monies. One was to establish a new Ming capital in Beijing, which began as the expeditions ended and turned out to be both magnificent and costly. This was the point at which the famous Forbidden City began to be constructed, [along with] a series of new tombs for the Ming emperors. These were costly investments, which arguably paid off in terms of the prestige of this new capital but certainly made it difficult to consider doing the two major enterprises at the same time. The other major investment was, of course, the reconstruction of the Great Wall. The concern about making sure the Mongols—now out—stayed out seemed to warrant this huge defensive investment. Obviously, the Great Wall is one of the famous architectural symbols of China, deservedly so. It was also extremely expensive. Again, it's hard to do too many things at once.

The ending of the Chinese expeditions did not end China's economic role in world trade. It did not isolate China from the rest of the world. These points we will need to return to, but obviously, the end of the expeditions did signal a terminus to the brief flurry of Chinese initiative going this far toward the rest of the world. Chinese activities, including merchant colonies in Southeast Asia, remained. They had been strengthened by the expeditions. There's a lingering impact here, but the extent of Chinese outreach that these expeditions had represented would frankly not be matched by China until the late 20th century. The decision to end the expeditions also re-raised the question that I started with: If the Chinese weren't going to organize the next interregional trade system, who would? The answer was obviously going to be clear fairly soon; we'll come back to it.

A second center of developments around 1450 involved the Middle East and southeast Europe. The decline of Arab rule had left openings for the immigration of new peoples from Central Asia, particularly Turkish people. Several waves had come in already. Turkish populations had been prominent in parts of the Middle East during the Crusades. Turks had been used in the administration of the later Abbasid caliphates. Turks were not new to the region, but around 1450, a new group of Turks, the Osmanli Turks, or Ottoman Turks, began to come in from Central Asia. Remember, they were already Muslims, actually quite fervent Muslims, heavily influenced by Sufism. They began to migrate into the area, and they began to be organized militarily, taking territories not only from Arab states, Arab rulers, but also increasingly focusing on attack on the Byzantine Empire. A major factor during the postclassical period in politics, trade, and obviously, cultural outreach, the Byzantine Empire had been declining considerably for some decades before 1450. Its territories shrunk. Increasingly finding it difficult to maintain the great city of Constantinople, the Byzantines were already in trouble, and obviously, this declining economic and political strength made them a ripe target for this new series of interlopers.

The Turks would lay siege to Constantinople. In 1453, the city fell, to be renamed by the Turks Istanbul, although the rest of the world acknowledged this name only more recently. The fall of Constantinople in 1453 is one of the great single events in world history, both for its real impact and its symbolic meaning. For the Middle East itself, it obviously represented a clear step—not a final step but a clear step—in the establishment of a new Turkish or, more properly, Ottoman Empire that would provide a new source of political and military power to a region that had been fragmented now for almost two centuries.

The fall of Constantinople also represented a new opportunity for the Turks and for Islam to move into the Balkans, to move into southeastern Europe. Already, even before the fall of Constantinople, the Turks had seized territories in parts of present-day Greece. The change to southeastern Europe was, in many ways, just as great as the impending change for parts of the Middle East. Russia was obviously hugely impacted. The Byzantine Empire had been the model for Russian development. The collapse of Constantinople, on the one hand, represented a rather terrifying challenge to Russian sense of identity, but it was also an equally liberating possibility because Russia could now see itself as inheriting a mission from the old Byzantine Empire, which would play some role in the new surge of Russia that we'll come back to in just a moment.

Finally, the fall of Constantinople was a symbolic and real challenge to other parts of Europe, including Western Europe. West Europeans, particularly Italians, had treated Constantinople very scornfully in the last days of the Byzantine Empire. As we've noted previously, one crusade actually invaded Constantinople directly in hopes [gaining] of plunder and reducing commercial competition. West Europeans did not pay any attention to appeals from late Byzantine emperors for assistance against the assailing Turks; they ignored them. But when the city fell, the sense of threat, the sense that a bastion of Christianity had been removed in favor of a new and fairly potent Islamic presence was something that Europeans had to grapple with quite directly, and it would take some time to assimilate. The Middle East, then, and southeastern Europe were a second center of change, along with the oscillations in Chinese economic activity and interregional policy.

Associated with the fall of Byzantium and the rise of the Turks was the extent to which the early 15th century represented the point at which Russian political rulers began fully to cast off Mongol rule. The process began to heat up around 1420. By 1450, as we've already noted, a real Russian state was forming around Moscow, and it was steadily expansionist. The fall of Byzantium was actually an additional spur to this Russian expansion. The Russian ruler carefully married one of the daughters of the last Byzantine emperor to maintain a clear link between a new Russian mission and the now failed Byzantine mission. We will have to come back to this important assertion of Russian power as it began to take shape around 1450, as well.

Not every place was changing in 1450, or not every place was changing massively. We've noted already that there was considerable basic continuity in Africa. African historians insist, of course, quite properly, that Africa must not be viewed as changeless. There were significant political shifts, alterations of trading patterns—the rise of the new kingdom of Songhai was an important development in the Sudanic region—but African stability, compared to developments elsewhere, I think, can be legitimately emphasized, as well.

Japan, of course, was digesting a certain degree of change. Again, we've noted earlier that the failure of the Mongol efforts to invade Japan, in contrast to their success in China, gave Japan a bit of food for thought and a new opportunity to rethink Japanese relationships, even with the Chinese. The year 1450 is not a striking point in Japanese development, but again, we need to remember that there was a bit of an adjustment going on in this case. Developments in India are not marked by any dramatic shifts around 1450. The more dramatic changes will come 50 or 70 years later with a new series of Islamic invasions into India. That's hovering in the wings but not yet there.

There were, however, by sheer coincidence—because, remember, there's no connection yet between American patterns and those elsewhere—significant developments in the Americas. Both the Aztecs and the Incas, by 1450, were beginning to encounter new challenges to their rule. Subject peoples were becoming more restive. The Inca Empire was probably overextended. Remember, its vast territory along a mountain stretch was very impressive but also hard to sustain. Quite spontaneously, quite independently of anything else, the great political structures of the late-postclassical period in the Americas were beginning to unravel to some extent. This would obviously facilitate European entry after 1492. No connection yet, but they need to be noted as simultaneous developments.

The final series of major developments occurred in new forms of European outreach. Beginning as early as the 13th century, individual European merchants and rulers had shown some interest in breaking the confines of European geography and its focus on the Mediterranean as an artery of trade. It was an artery of trade [that] inevitably led to interaction with and dependence on Islamic merchants and Islamic centers of power. In the 13th century, a Genoan expedition set out into the Atlantic. Obviously, the Atlantic was potentially the great escape hatch. We have no idea what happened to it; they never came back. But the fact that they went is actually an interesting revelation. Farther to the north, of course, Scandinavians had crossed the Atlantic. Scandinavians had successfully reached North America, found nothing they particularly valued there, and retreated to more interesting and durable settlements in Greenland and, particularly, Iceland. There's a bridge in the north, but it's not one that connects particularly to developments in the 14th and 15th centuries.

By the early 15th century, patterns of exploration in the Atlantic, down the African coast, were beginning to extend quite routinely. This was sponsored particularly by the king of Portugal, newly freed from Muslim control, but with some interest also by rulers in Spain—where, also, Islamic control was being pushed back. The last Islamic enclave in Granada would fall in Spain in 1492, an interesting coincidence of dates. The explorations steadily pushed down the African coast. The purpose was, "Let's see what we can find. Maybe there are great sources of gold." An understanding that Africa had considerable gold supplies and myths about even greater riches were rampant in Europe at this point. There was a clear mercenary twinge. The larger framework, remember, was a European recognition that it did face some clear difficulties in the interregional relationships that had developed during the postclassical period. European taste for Asian goods—upper-class taste, primarily—was well established. There's a consumer stake here; there's money to be made.

But at the same time, the European capacity to pay for these goods was not terribly well established. By seeking new sources of gold, by seeking other opportunities, the Europeans were obviously trying to remedy what was just, front and center, a clear problem in their interregional outreach. They also began to wonder if by pressing down Africa, they could find a direct connection with Asia itself. Thus, they would save money by avoiding the Islamic middlemen and save cultural challenge by bypassing Islam in favor of connections with Asia directly. This interest in, again, a combination of a cultural and economic solution to the problems of dependence on Islamic merchants, this effort to find a solution, was galvanized further by the fall of Constantinople—by the sense of a new level, a new potential for Muslim organization in the eastern Mediterranean. The spur here was considerable.

The conventional textbooks on West European history obviously emphasize the background to these new expeditions in a somewhat different fashion. There's no reason that we have to choose fully between them. It was certainly true that, by 1450, European political capacity was beginning to improve. There was still a great deal of internal warfare. Indeed, the great Hundred Years War between England and France was still raging. But in England, France, and now, increasingly, Spain and Portugal, European monarchies or feudal monarchies had managed to achieve a bit more central control over their territories. They did have a somewhat greater capacity to guide trade policy and to do things such as mount significant exploratory expeditions. European Christianity, not a new force, may have been given a new lease on life in terms of missionary spirit by the success of driving the Muslims out of the Iberian Peninsula. Sometimes this kind of success will help promote a further sense of great zeal. Spanish and, to a lesser degree, Portuguese Catholic leaders were prominent in playing roles in the explorations that began to take shape in the 15th century. A motive of religious conversion, associated with a desire to push Muslims farther back from Europe, may have been a spur here. Certainly, we need to acknowledge that 1450 was a point in which new attitudes in the Renaissance were developing—first in Italy and, by 1450, beginning to spread more widely. The Renaissance did suggest a new level of attention to activities on this Earth, rather than simply religious motivations. They did suggest some new confidence in the possibilities of individual achievement. It's no accident that some of the great explorers would turn out to be Italian, the center of the Renaissance.

I think the world history picture has to continue to be more complicated. The European expeditions down Africa may have had some religious motivation, although the commercial/economic motivation was much stronger at the outset. There may have been some Renaissance spirit involved, but the sense of key problems to be solved, the sense of the need to deal with the problem of the Islamic intermediary, and the sense of the need to compensate for the new Islamic control in the eastern Mediterranean—these spurs were very real, as well.

Still, around 1450—a bit before, extending to a bit after—as the expeditions unfolded, they also revealed a couple of other points that I think bring us back to the complexity of the motivations involved. First of all, the expeditions for all their hopes, failed to find massive troves of new wealth. They did, however, find some new territories. Europeans began to take over island groups in the southern Atlantic, such as the Azores and the Canaries. When they arrived in these island groups, several things happened. First of all, they didn't find

©2007 The Teaching Company

gold, so that was a disappointment. They did find a native population, however, that had been long removed from contact with Europe. The Romans had been vaguely aware of these island groups, but there had been no active exchange for a long time. These population groups were extremely vulnerable to some of the common diseases the Europeans brought, such as measles and smallpox. A rapid depopulation occurred in these islands, which was at once a useful development for the Europeans—local resistance was minimal—but also a challenge because there was the obvious need to think about finding additional sources of labor.

The solution adopted, again in the 15th century, was to begin to raid the northwest African mainland for sources of slaves. Slavery was a well-established system in Africa; there were African merchants willing to play ball. The Europeans began importing African slaves into these island groups with the purpose of establishing sugar cultivation. Remember, one of the great European interests in interregional trade was the acquisition of sugar, the indulgence of a Western sweet tooth. If the new territories did not yield the kind of easy wealth that the Europeans hoped for, they could at least yield opportunities to reduce dependence on sugar imports directly from Asia. Sugar plantations were established in these island groups using slave labor, cleared obviously by the fact that new diseases had carried off the local population. Obviously, something of a dress rehearsal—not planned but something of a dress rehearsal—was being developed that would prefigure what would later happen in the Americas when the Europeans reached there.

An obvious further point is that this kind of policy is, I think, perfectly understandable in terms of European interest. They had an economic problem, they wanted to resolve it, and growing sugar directly was one at least partial remedy. This European policy of economic exploitation and seizure of slaves did raise some interesting questions about what would be the nature of the European role in the world as Europeans, beginning with these expeditions, gained new levels of power. The comparison with earlier groups of global overlords, such as Arabs and Mongols, is interesting and not always to the West's clear advantage.

The other thing, of course—and I've mentioned this before—that the Europeans learned, not in 1450 but a little bit later, was that once they did actually succeed in rounding the southern tip of Africa and reaching Asia directly, they still had a problem. Remember, Vasco da Gama's first expedition around the Cape of Good Hope and to India revealed that the Europeans still, although they now had some direct contact, had a balance-of-payments problem. Da Gama did not carry with him much, except some gold, that was useful in exchange with Asia. When da Gama went back—and now we're after 1500—he brought with him a solution. The solution was military; he brought guns. He deliberately slaughtered a number of Indian officials as examples to the rest of the population that they should become willing to trade, even though the Europeans did not yet have very much to offer in the exchange. Again, it's an interesting prefiguring of developments that would occur later.

The key point, in concluding about 1450, is to emphasize the variety of developments that were occurring and the number of different places that were involved. There's no tidy pattern. To be sure, the Chinese expeditions and their end help set a stage where, fairly soon, European initiatives would prove to be the new basis for a framework for interregional trade. But Chinese policy decisions and European adventures are only part of the story. Developments in the Middle East, the arrival of the Turks, the fall of one of the great Christian empires, and the beginning of new assertions by Russians as they pushed the Mongols back—all of these developments need to be factored in, as well. Not surprisingly, the end of the postclassical period was complicated. It did ultimately involve the gradual emergence of a new system of interregional trade that would be immensely important, but it also involved power and cultural shifts in other regions. A complicated period in world history ended in a complicated fashion and set the stage for a rich but not straightforward pattern of development in world history's next period.

Lecture Nineteen
The Early Modern Period, 1450–1750

Scope:

The most important development in this new period of world history involved the rise of international trade and the redefinition of this trade to include the entire globe for the first time. Western Europe was a key agent in much of this change, including the new contacts with the Americas and, at the end of the period, with Pacific Oceania and Australia. The conventional emphasis for the period, in terms of a fascination with growing European strength and changes within Europe itself, is accurate but should not overshadow the broader patterns of change. European dominance of the Americas and its new influence in Africa are qualified by a much more complicated relationship with most of Asia. A final theme for the period—what historians often call the age of *gunpowder empires*—calls attention not only to the emergence of Europe's overseas colonies but also to the rise of several new land-based agglomerations in Asia. The early modern period thus focuses on new patterns of trade and new exchanges, along with a new spurt of empire formation from several sources. Strong elements of this new global economic system persist today. Interestingly, the period is not defined by any overall patterns of cultural change, despite significant developments in particular regions.

Outline

I.   The early modern period in world history runs roughly from 1450 to 1750.

    A. In contrast to the classical and postclassical periods (lasting 1,500 and 1,000 years, respectively), the early modern period is relatively short (300 years).

        1. One explanation for this shorter time span may be that the pace of change became more rapid.

        2. As we get closer to the present we have more abundant records.

        3. We also tend to spend more time on periods that are closer to the present because, inevitably, they have more influence on current patterns of activity.

B. Some historians would argue that 1500 is a better date for the start of the early modern period.

   1. By 1500, it was clear that the Europeans would introduce significant changes in the Americas.

   2. By 1500, the Ottoman Empire had expanded from southwestern Europe and the northeastern Middle East to include portions of North Africa, especially Egypt.

C. The end of the period, 1750, is a date of convenience meant to indicate the coming changes brought on by European industrialization.

D. The early modern period is where many world history educational programs go awry, focusing on European power after 1450 and the glories of change in the West. This view distorts and oversimplifies the continued complexity of the world as a whole.

   1. We must recognize that the power of Western Europe did increase and that the nature of the West itself was significantly transformed.

   2. That said, Europe did not run the world in 1750: many societies, continued to act independently of Europe, and important developments occurred that had very little to do with Europe.

II. In establishing a new period in history, we must show that the previously predominant themes have lost some force.

A. The postclassical period was defined by expansion in the geographical range, the number of civilizations, the impact of the world religions, and the establishment of a world network connecting different parts of Africa, Asia, and Europe.

   1. Because the main contours of the civilization zones were fairly well established, expansion was no longer a dominating principle.

   2. For the world as a whole, the religious map was fairly well established.

   3. The world network was still an operative concept but was transformed by of the inclusion of the Americas. The earlier network was an intense interrelationship among different societies in what we might call the Old

World; the new world economy is global and even more intense.

B. What, then, are the new themes?

    1. The most important developments in the early modern period are the intensification of interregional trade connections and the inclusion of the Americas (and later Pacific Oceania).

    2. Other new themes include the new power relationship of the West in the world, the biological exchanges that resulted from European and African contact with the Americas, and the "explosion" of gunpowder empires.

III. Carlo Cipolla sums up the expansion of Europe in the title of his book, *Guns, Sails, and Empires.*

A. By the 15th century, Europeans had adapted Chinese explosive powder for use in guns, particularly cannons. The technology for casting church bells was transferred to casting bronze and iron cannons.

B. Sails came from adaptations of Arab shipping, and Europeans learned how to make more effective oceangoing vessels, which proved to be particularly successful in navigating the waters of the Atlantic and then the Pacific; at the same time there was an increasing use of navigational devices such as the compass.

C. Guns and sails in this period took Europeans to islands and coastal regions where they could establish oceangoing contact and use their sea-based cannons to intimidate and threaten.

    1. Europeans seized port cities in West Africa and occasionally East Africa, some ports in India, island groups in what is now Indonesia, territory in Taiwan, and the Philippines.

    2. With rare exceptions, the interior of Africa and Asia would remain immune to European conquest at this point.

D. In the Americas, Europeans had the added advantage of metal tools and technologies, horses, and military organization that, in some instances, was superior to that of the Native American peoples.

E. The Europeans also had the "advantage" of disease. Up to 80 or 85 percent of the total Native American population died off from disease within two centuries. This cleared the way for European conquest as no other development could.

F. With regard to the European weapons and naval advantages, we might well ask why no other society in the early modern period chose to rival the Europeans in this game.

    1. Several other societies had metalworking traditions, shipbuilding capabilities, as well as experience in interregional activity, but chose not to imitate the European patterns of expansion.

    2. The Chinese had no use for such expansion primarily because it did not serve the purposes of Chinese society itself.

    3. The case is similar in Japan. In the 16th century, the Japanese were especially interested in new types of European weapons but at the end of the century they cut off European contacts, partly because Catholic control in the Philippines was viewed as a threat and European weapons endangered the system of feudalism.

G. The sense that European patterns were not relevant to the goals of key societies motivated a distinctive stance toward European technology. Europeans, in turn, viewed themselves as having a technological edge over the new societies they came in contact with and began to judge other societies mainly by the state of their technology.

IV. Another key development in this period involved what historians routinely call the *Colombian exchange*. This term refers to the fact that biological products moved from the Americas to the rest of the world and vice versa, an exchange that was almost entirely disastrous for the Americas.

A. Biological exchange meant that Old World domesticated animals were brought to the Americas, as were Old World food products.

B. Unfortunately, the main biological import to the Americas was disease. At first, the impact was accidental, though by the 18th and 19th centuries, Europeans deliberately introduced diseases into Native American populations in order to clear them out.

C. The Colombian exchange for other parts of the world was arguably beneficial; American food products began to spread widely to other areas, helping to sustain and even augment populations

D. African involvement in the Colombian exchange was complicated. New World foods, particularly corn, spread widely to Africa and helped sustain population development. But another biological exchange took the form of people themselves moving to the Americas.

    1. Beginning in the 16th century, 8–12 million Africans would be seized in the Atlantic slave trade and taken to the Americas.

    2. This level of displacement had serious consequences for Africa—particularly West Africa—because a disproportionate number of the slaves were young males at a prime age for reproduction.

E. The most vigorous impact of the Colombian exchange had ended by the early-18th century. People became more resistant to disease in the Americas, and the bulk of the population was now of mixed European and Native American heritage.

V. The early modern period is also known as the age of gunpowder empires.

A. The Europeans, led by the Spanish and Portuguese and followed by the Dutch, British, and French, established their overseas empires in the Americas and in parts of Asia and Africa.

B. Equally important was the establishment of land-based gunpowder empires in Asia.

    1. The Ottoman Turks, for example, had used gunpowder and cannon in their siege of Constantinople and established their empire partly based on this technology.

    2. The Mughal Empire in India was also organized by invaders using new weaponry.

    3. The Safavid Empire in Persia and the Russian Empire were based in part on gunpowder.

C. The new empires that arose in Eastern Europe and much of Asia were quite different in orientation from the more commercially minded overseas empires but equally important because they maintained sway over a significant landmass and dynamic economies.

D. Even in China, the Qing dynasty, launched in the 17th century by Manchurians, was partly a gunpowder empire.

VI. We can pinpoint a few social and cultural areas where we do not see major developments in this period.

A. The early modern era is not a distinct period with regard to gender relationships, although we can see some changes.

  1. The arrival of Europeans in the Americas had implications for American gender relations because European values and expectations differed greatly from Native American traditions.

  2. In withdrawing men from Africa, the slave trade increased the importance of polygamy to provide family arrangements for the remaining women.

  3. There is no blanket pattern, however, that allows us to use the early modern period for purposes of gender discrimination.

B. In the same way, culture in the early modern period reveals changes in specific cases but no blanket pattern.

  1. The importation of European religion, artistic styles, and some science to the Americas was a major change in American cultural history.

  2. European culture would also change with, for example, the rise of science and the division of West European Christendom.

  3. In the world as a whole in the early modern period, however, there is no overall cultural dynamic: individual societies, such as Japan or China, would indulge new opportunities for contact to a degree but not at the expense of substantial cultural differentiation.

VII. Let us close by reviewing the main themes of the early modern period.

    A. The rise of Europe was accompanied by the establishment of significant political units in other parts of the world that would long overshadow Western politics.

    B. The biological exchange that resulted from the inclusion of the Americas in the world network prompted various reactions.

        1. Many societies had to make decisions about how to handle new contacts with the West, including whether they would make use of new foods.

        2. They also had to make decisions about the impact of new imperial structures, land-based as well as sea-based.

    C. The central theme in this period was the intensification of economic relationships, which now also included the Americas and, at the end of the period, parts of the Pacific.

    D. One interpretation of this period argues that the West managed to position itself as a transmitter of American goods, and this transmission served as the engine of the world economy with much more diverse benefits and implications than we usually think of when we look at the rise of the West alone.

Further Reading:

Carlo Cipolla, *Guns, Sails, and Empires: Technological Innovation and the Early Phases of European Expansion, 1400–1700.*

Michael Adas, *Machines as the Measure of Men: Science, Technology, and Ideologies of Western Dominance.*

Noel Perrin, *Giving Up the Gun: Japan's Reversion to the Sword.*

Jeffrey Pilcher, *Food in World History.*

Questions to Consider:

1. How did growing Western dominance compare with previous Middle Eastern dominance of world trade? Were Western policies harsher or more benign in their impacts on other societies?

2. Why did the rise of the West not generate wider interest in Western cultural forms during the early modern period?

Lecture Nineteen—Transcript
The Early Modern Period, 1450–1750

Today, we'll be talking about the early modern period in world history, a period that runs roughly 1450–1750, the next period after the great postclassical millennium. The period warrants two comments by way of general introduction. First, it's obviously very short. We've been dealing with 1,500 years for the classical period, 1,000 for the postclassical, and now we're talking about 300. The reasons for this are probably threefold, and I won't even pretend to say which is most important. First of all, change may have speeded up. That's a modern impression, and maybe it's true. I'm honestly not sure, but it's worth thinking about. Second, as we get closer to the present, we know more; there are more abundant records. That's pretty obvious, but it also helps historians feed larger sections of their treatments. Third, I think quite legitimately, you need to spend more time on periods that are closer to the present day because, inevitably, they will have even more influence on current patterns of activity. These [are] connections we'll be working on through the discussions from this point onward, but they're perfectly legitimate. This is a perfectly honest, indeed useful, employment of historical analysis.

The period begins in 1450 or so. We talked last time about some of the components that were changing in the world in 1450, including the new European expeditions, the significant changes in the Middle East and Eastern Europe, and the Chinese decision, which helped set the stage for new activity, as well. Some historians would urge [that] maybe 1500 is a bit better date. By 1500, it was becoming clear that the Europeans had arrived in the Americas and were actually going to utilize their arrival to introduce significant changes—that, obviously, was not even on the horizon clearly in 1450. Also by 1500, the Ottoman Empire had expanded from its hold in southwestern Europe-northeastern Middle East to include victories over Egyptian forces that extended the Ottoman Empire through much of the Arab world—not all of it but much of it—including portions of North Africa, with Egypt obviously front and center.

The years 1450–1500 get things started. At the other end, 1750 is frankly a date of convenience. It really is used mainly to say, well, it's around this time that things are going to be changing because of the impact of European industrialization. It's not an entirely satisfactory decision; we'll have to talk about it when we talk about the next period in world history. This is an unusual case in which the boundaries of a period at the end are, frankly, pretty vague—but let's be honest, that's the way it's usually done.

Early modern, obviously, is meant to be revealing. It's not quite modern, hence *early*, but it's a lot more recognizable in terms of our world today than the postclassical was. It's a term that was long used in European history. I don't think it's a distortion to use it in world history, but we need to recognize what some of the implications are.

The second general comment about the early modern period is really a warning. This is where many well-intentioned world history educational programs go off the rails, for example, the California state system. California establishes elegant parameters for world history up through 1450. They offer interesting treatments of Islam, of Asia, of Africa, etc., but then in 1450, the world becomes Europe and two things happen. One: the expansion of European power—which is undeniable—becomes the central theme, so that everything is organized around how societies were reached by Europe and how they reacted to Europe, as though they had no independent volition or background. That just oversimplifies and distorts. The second thing that happens is that European history is suddenly given a richness; we're indulging ourselves in looking at the glories of changes in the West, as if nothing else were going on elsewhere, as if these developments need to receive a degree of attention that simply distracts from the continued complexity of the world as a whole.

In dealing with the early modern period, we must recognize that the power of Western Europe in the world did increase. That's a legitimate major change. We must recognize that the nature of the West itself was significantly transformed in ways that were obviously important in the West and would have implications for other regions. But we must keep balance. I think it's easy to do, but we need to keep the warning in mind. Europe did not run the world in 1750. Many societies continued to act in great independence of Europe. Important developments continued to occur that had very little to do with Europe one way or another. The world continued to be complicated; the world continued to operate along several parallel lines.

In establishing a new period, as we discussed when we talked about the introduction of the postclassical period, we need not only to have a set of dates—here 1450 or so, 1750 or so—we also have to have a fairly clear sense that the themes that had previously predominated have lost some force. This is, actually, fairly easy to state. The postclassical period—lots of things going on—was defined above all by a clear expansion in the geographical range and number of civilizations, by the impact of the world religions, and by the establishment of a world network connecting different parts of Africa, Asia, and Europe. The theme of expansion of civilization can obviously continue to be played in the early modern period, but because the main contours of the civilization zones are pretty well established—particularly outside of the Americas—it's no longer a dominant organizing principle. World religions did continue to expand. Islam is still moving into Southeast Asia. Obviously, the Ottoman conquests introduced the possibility of a significant Muslim minority in southeastern Europe, as well. Christianity would expand hugely in the Americas during the early modern period, although not quite as rapidly as some priests and monks had hoped. But for the world as a whole, the religious map was pretty well set, and the big impact of world religions really had come and gone in terms of a major innovative force. Their sustaining power is still there; the world network simply gets transformed. It's still an operative concept, but it gets transformed because of the inclusion of the Americas. The world network was an intense interrelationship among different societies in what we might conveniently call the Old World. The New World economy—which we'll explore more fully next time—is literally global, and that's a huge change.

Now we turn to the most important part—what are the new themes? Indeed, the most important single development in the early modern period is the intensification of interregional trade connections and the inclusion of the Americas—at the very end of the period, the inclusion also of Pacific Oceania—in these global trade patterns. It was a huge development, pretty obviously, and the implications are immense.

Other changes and new themes include—and these are what we're going to explore during the balance of our discussion today—the new power relationship of the West in the world—it didn't happen overnight; it has to be seen as gradual, but it did occur—the biological exchanges that resulted from European and African contact with the Americas; and finally, the explosion—no pun intended—of gunpowder empires. It's a point that relates to the expansion of Europe but needs separate attention.

First, let's discuss the expansion of Europe. This can be very simply summed up—and there's a nice book by Carlo Cipolla precisely along these lines—as guns, sails, and empires. By the 15th century, Europeans had adapted Chinese explosive powder into guns and, particularly, cannon. They benefited interestingly from the fact that, well before the advent of Chinese explosive powder in Europe, Europeans were already familiar with heavy metal casting, interestingly, for the purpose of making church bells. Now, nobody sat around when church bells were being developed saying, "Say, I think several centuries from now this will make a great weapon," but the fact is [this was] another bit of dumb luck. Europeans were able to transfer this technology to the casting of bronze and iron cannon. Sails came from adaptations of Arab shipping. Europeans learned how to make more effective oceangoing vessels. They stopped depending on galley slaves to row through the Mediterranean. These new vessels proved to be particularly successful in navigating the waters of the Atlantic and then the Pacific. Along with guns and sails came, of course, the increasing utilization of navigational devices, most of which the Europeans had borrowed from elsewhere—the compass, etc.—and the Europeans were off and running.

For the most part, guns and sails in the early modern period took Europeans mainly to islands and coastal regions where they could establish oceangoing contact and use their sea-based cannon to intimidate and threaten. Thus, Europeans, over the early modern period, seized some port cities in West Africa and, occasionally, a bit in East Africa, though the European presence was much less significant there. They seized some ports in India, such as the Portuguese port of Goa, which was only given back to India a few years ago. They seized island groups in what's now Indonesia. They periodically seized territory in Taiwan. They certainly seized the Philippines. These were places where ships, ships' cannon, and short distance expeditions from ships would pay off particularly well. It's obviously vital to recognize—no mystery—that with rare exceptions, the interior of Africa and Asia would remain immune to European conquest at this point. The technology was simply not relevant. Europeans made inroads in African territories directly only

©2007 The Teaching Company

in Angola, a Portuguese holding, and then a bit later on in South Africa, where the Dutch established a foothold. But otherwise, their dealings with Africa in terms of the use of ships and force are coastal, as is the case with most of Asia.

The huge exception, of course, was the Americas, where Europeans had the advantage not just of ships and guns—though this was certainly relevant—but also metal tools and technologies, horses, and a sense of military organization that, in some instances at least, was superior to that which had been developed among Native American peoples. The European conquest of the Americas was gradual. Let's not assume that Europeans suddenly, because they made huge land claims over South America, for example, seized these territories fully. European success here was absolutely vital, but in terms of the world as a whole, atypical. Remember, it was accompanied by another advantage the Europeans had—if advantage is the right word—that they did not have with regard to Asia and Africa. That was the advantage of disease. The decimation of American populations because of imported diseases, running up to 80–85 percent of the total Native American population dying off within two centuries—whole populations in some cases, literally, entirely extinguished; minorities remaining in other instances—this cleared the way for European conquest as no other development could. The expansion of Europe and the establishment of European military presence was mainly a naval activity, underwritten by new technologies that had developed as Europe encountered Asian societies and utilized the contacts to their own benefit. It was developed in different ways in the Americas because of the very special circumstances that resulted, frankly primarily, from previous American isolation.

A question obviously arises with regard to this European weapons advantage as to why no other society in the early modern period decided to rival the Europeans at their own game. It's a valid question. Several societies, doubtless, could have done so because they had the metalworking traditions, they had the shipbuilding capacity, and they had experience in interregional activity, but they did not do so. The Chinese, for example, although abundantly exposed to European example and interested in some European artifacts—for example, clocks—decided not to imitate European patterns at this point. This was probably partly because of a

Confucian reluctance to indulge too many activities that would give greater prestige to merchant values and merchant life. It was also probably because of a bureaucratic suspicion of too much change occurring all at once. Above all, it was because China simply had no use for these patterns in terms of the purposes seen for Chinese society itself. As we will see more fully in a later discussion, China benefited hugely from Europe's world economy. Because of the Chinese productive capacity, they didn't need to emulate European weapons patterns and naval patterns in order to seize these benefits. China was interested in maintaining the integrity of the Middle Kingdom against outside invasion. European devices here, particularly naval devices, were of little use. The Chinese proved perfectly capable of organizing their contacts with Europeans through some regulated ports, particularly the port of Macao. They simply did not have problems that European weapons patterns would seem to solve.

Something of the same case applies to Japan, although we know a little bit more about debates in this regard. As Europeans first encountered Japan in the 16th century, the Japanese were initially rather interested in what the Europeans had to offer. There were even some significant conversions to Christianity. Japan was, after all, a warlike, feudal society, and seeing a people with new types of weapons could be a real turn-on. There was considerable interest in European guns and a quick capacity to manufacture similar types of guns in Japan itself. But at the end of the 16th century, under a ruler named Hideyoshi, the Japanese made a decision to cut off these contacts and to end this degree of interest in European weapons patterns. The decision was motivated, first, by a realization of what the Europeans were doing to the Philippines, a sense that European control of the Philippines in the name of the pope—or so the Japanese viewed it—would be so threatening to the Japanese culture and value system, that the threat simply could not be endured. Japan needed to cut off contact, lest what happened to the Philippines happen there.

Second, it was clearly realized that while eagerness for European weapons might be a delightful edge for feudal belligerence in the short term, in the long term, European weapons would threaten the system of feudalism itself. Older fighting patterns were essential to maintain feudal values and feudal social relationships. This maintenance was more important than the opportunities that the

Europeans seemed to offer. Japan cut off this kind of interest and regulated the manufacture of guns. In some years in the 17th century, Japan produced only nine guns per year. This was simply not going to be a dominant pattern for the Japanese political and military system.

The sense that European patterns, although obviously extremely dynamic, were not relevant to the goals of key societies, a sense of social preservation or cultural preservation or both, motivated a stance toward European technology that was obviously very distinct. Europeans, in turn, quickly developed a sense that whatever their drawbacks with regard to the new societies they were in contact with—in the opulence of cities, the richness of tradition—at least they had a technology edge. Europeans began to judge other societies mainly by the state of technology and, obviously, in the process, found their own society vastly superior. It's an interesting pattern of evaluation that I think still operates in much of the contemporary world.

Along with the rise of Europe and its military base, a second key development involved what historians routinely call the *Colombian exchange*. Here's where the biological entry of the Americas into the global system had its clear expression. The Colombian exchange means that biological products moved from the Americas to the rest of the world and from the rest of the world to the Americas. The exchange for the Americas themselves was almost entirely disastrous. Obviously, biological exchange meant that Old World domesticated animals were brought to the Americas, and Americans proved very adept at using horses, for example, in this new system. Old World food products, such as wheat and other grains, were also brought to the Americas, where they would embellish the food supply. But the big import biologically to the Americas was disease and, as we've already seen, it had horrendous impact. The impact was accidental. Europeans and Africans did not intend to bring these diseases to the Americas. Though, over time, by the 18th and 19th centuries, Europeans actually learned deliberately to introduce diseases into Native American populations in order to clear them out. It was initially accidental; it became sometimes intentional.

The Colombian exchange for other parts of the world was arguably beneficial. Beneficial may be a slightly loaded word [here], but beneficial may do. That is, American food products began to spread widely to other areas and enhance food supplies in ways that would help sustain and even augment populations. China, for example, by the early 17th century, was utilizing American crops, such as sweet potatoes and corn, along with some new strains of rice in China. This served as a basis for considerable population expansion later in the 17th and 18th centuries. China gained these crops mainly through their ongoing contact with the Philippines, where Spaniards had introduced European crops to see if they would also help improve the food supply there. The pattern obviously shows the continued complexity of China's relationship with the wider world and the capacity for real innovation. India also adopted some New World crops and, again, there were probably population consequences there, as well. Europe, ironically, was slower to introduce New World crops. Europeans were very food conservative, arguing that these new crops were not mentioned in the Bible and, therefore, might be the source of evil and disease. But by the late 17th century, Europeans as well were beginning to use the potato—corn, less, which remained mainly a food for animals—and, on this basis, would experience a dramatic population increase, as well. The Colombian exchange for the world as a whole served to augment the food basis for population growth, but in particular societies, particularly the Americas themselves, served as a population deterrent for a considerable period of time.

The African involvement in the Colombian exchange was obviously complicated. New World foods, particularly corn, spread widely to Africa and helped sustain population development, but here, there was another biological exchange in people themselves that worked in the other direction. Beginning in the 16th century, 8–12 million Africans would be seized in the Atlantic slave trade and taken to the Americas, often in hideous conditions. It was a level of displacement that had obvious population consequences for Africa—particularly West Africa—as a disproportionate number of the slaves were males and young, at a prime age for reproduction. Overall, in the early modern period, when these two forces are put together, African populations roughly stabilized, suffering in some regions and benefiting slightly in others.

The most vigorous impact of the Colombian exchange had ended by the early 18th century. Disease patterns began to stabilize in the Americas as more people became disease-resistant. The bulk of the population was now mixed European and Native American heritage in the Mestizo group that would quickly become a majority. The Colombian exchange is not an eternal pattern in world history, but it did organize some very significant developments during much of the early modern period, some of which, including China's population growth, would continue to ramify thereafter.

The third basic feature of the early modern period was the extent to which gunpowder was utilized to establish a new series of empires in a way that actually had never before been matched in world history. This was a great age of empire at two levels. The first is familiar. The Europeans, launched by the Spanish and Portuguese, had established their famous overseas empires in the Americas and in parts of Asia and Africa, as we've already discussed. Spanish, Portuguese, Dutch, British, and French empires become the great overseas empires of the early modern period, with huge consequences in world history. Equally important—indeed, for much of the early modern period, more important—was the establishment of land-based gunpowder empires in Asia. The Ottoman Turks, for example, had used gunpowder and cannon in their siege of Constantinople. The establishment of the Ottoman Empire was partly based on the use of land-based cannon and guns. The new Mughal Empire in India was similarly organized by invaders who utilized new weaponry. The Safavid Empire in Persia was another gunpowder empire. The expanded Russian Empire quickly became a fourth gunpowder empire.

In Eastern Europe and much of Asia, a new series of empires arose on the basis of new military technology. They were quite different in orientation from the more commercially minded overseas empires but equally important because they maintained sway over such a significant landmass and over such dynamic economies. Even in China, the last dynasty, which launched in the 17th century, the Qing dynasty, was itself partly a gunpowder empire operated by Manchurians, not Chinese proper. They used new weaponry as one of their means of obtaining new political control on the Chinese mainland. This establishment of empire, which goes way beyond the familiar story of the rise of the West, is a crucial development in the early modern period that deserves attention in its own right.

A couple of things did not happen in world history in this period. The early modern period is not a distinct period with regard to gender relationships, for example. With the complicated impact of the world religions on gender relations—but also the pattern of increasing subservience of women in a number of key societies, such as China—the postclassical period suggests a break in gender relations. In terms of the world as a whole, the early modern period did not. There were important developments. The arrival of Europeans in the Americas had huge implications for American gender relations because European values and expectations differed so greatly from Native American traditions. The slave trade, in withdrawing men from Africa, increased the importance of polygamy in Africa because of the need to provide family arrangements for the remaining women. Again, it was a significant gender change. There are points of change in specific cases, but there's no blanket pattern that allows us to use the early modern period for purposes of gender discrimination.

The same thing, interestingly, applies to culture. There are all sorts of cultural developments in the early modern period, and we will have to pay attention to them. The importation of European religion, artistic styles, and some science to the Americas was a huge change in American cultural history. European culture itself would change— and we'll be taking this up quite specifically—with, for example, the rise of science, the division of European Christendom, etc. European cultural patterns would have some impact on a few other societies, particularly Russia, but in the world as a whole in the early modern period, there is no overall cultural dynamic. It's as though—and I think in some cases this is really exactly the situation—individual societies, such as Japan, even as new opportunities for contact developed, decided, okay, we may indulge these to a degree— perhaps China would be a better example here—but not at the expense of massive cultural influence. The Chinese, for example, would tolerate a little bit of European missionary activity as long as the Europeans were respectful of Chinese ways and dressed as Confucian scholars, but they were not interested in more significant cultural interpenetration. Indeed, they would later move to block missionary activity to a greater extent, as well. This is not a period of vibrant cultural exchange on a global basis; this is not a period of systematic cultural innovation.

The main points in the early modern period are to recognize the obvious—that a number of different things are going on. The rise of Europe is a real fact. It doesn't have the same implications for some parts of the world as it does for others, but it's a real fact. Along with the rise of the West comes the establishment of really significant political units in other parts of the world that would long overshadow Western politics per se. Along with these political developments came the force of the biological exchange, which results from the inclusion of the Americas. There are a number of things going on that would prompt reactions from different societies. Many societies did have to make some decisions about how to handle new contacts with the West, and these decisions varied, but they also had to make decisions about the utilization of new foods and reactions to new diseases. They also had to make decisions about the impact of new imperial structures, land-based as well as sea-based. A lot was going on, and different regions would react differently.

Here is one final point. I mentioned—and it really needs to be repeated—that, along with the specifics—the gunpowder empires, the Colombian exchange, etc.—we need to keep in mind the central theme. That central theme was the intensification of economic relationships, which now also included the Americas and, at the end of the period, parts of the Pacific, in ways that would have deep impact. As one final caution against placing too much emphasis on Western achievements in this whole pattern, one interpretation argues that what the West really managed in the early modern period was to place itself as a transmitter of American goods. It was this transmission that actually served as the engine of the world economy, with much more diverse benefits and implications than we usually think of when we think of the rise of the West alone.

Lecture Twenty
The World Economy, 1450–1750

Scope:

In the early modern period, world trade increased, becoming literally global and seeing an increasingly powerful role for the West. Above all, trade became more important to many societies, helping to shape not only economic life but political and social systems as well. With the growing importance of trade in such products as slaves, sugar, silver, guns, and elite craft items, a number of societies began to develop elaborate relationships of superiority and dependence. Western Europe became the superior player: it had strong governments and a flexible wage labor system, and it emphasized manufactured products such as guns or luxury furnishings, that could earn top money in world trade. The West carried the trade in its ships and commercial companies, other sources of profit. On the other hand, peripheral societies exported cheap foods and raw materials, using coercive labor to cut costs (and to respond to labor shortages), relying on merchant companies and ships from the European core, and importing more expensive items. Weak governments followed from the lack of an ample tax base, the interference of the West, and the desire of landlords to regulate their own labor forces. Wealth flowed from the periphery to the Western core. Latin America, the Caribbean, and the North American South were the classic peripheries, but West Africa, with its slave trade, had peripheral characteristics. By the 18th century, grain-exporting regions such as Poland, which relied on serf labor, were becoming peripheries also. The biggest problem with the world economy approach, for the early modern period, involves the continuing success of Asian economies, headed by China. We will take this complexity into account as we discuss the world economy.

Outline

I. The main development underlying all others in the early modern period was the intensification of world economic relationships and the inclusion of the Americas in those relationships.

©2007 The Teaching Company

A. When we discussed the world network in the postclassical period, we mentioned that it was capable of affecting basic manufacturing patterns, as in China, for example. When we look at the early modern period, we see the same kind of intensification operating at a higher level in a set of different economies.

B. Immanuel Wallerstein, an American sociologist, developed *world economy theory* to explain this intensification; the theory is a useful device for exploring relationships in the early modern period and even in the present day.

C. In addition to illustrating general points about intensification, world economy theory has three advantages.

    1. It clarifies systematic inequalities in international economic relationships that emerged in the early modern period and, thus, helps explain why societies otherwise as different as Latin America and Poland can be viewed through something of the same lens.

    2. It deals with relationships between export and import activities within societies, economic position in the world economy, and political structures and labor systems.

    3. It helps to explain why certain patterns endure for so long and why they are hard to eliminate.

D. We should note, however, that world economy theory has been widely criticized for omitting certain factors (such as culture and technology) and for oversimplifying some points. The theory also has difficulty in dealing with change and does not do justice to the complexity of patterns in Asia

II. Wallerstein introduces four key concepts, three of which we will discuss in this lecture.

A. He identifies core and peripheral societies—the "winners" and "losers" in the early modern world economy. Because not all societies were fully enmeshed in the world economy at this point, Wallerstein also brings in external societies, in which the economy is not primarily dependent on global relationships.

B. Wallerstein argues that these economic relationships—particularly the crucial duo of core/periphery—are born with the early modern period. Although elements of these relationships existed in the postclassical period, they become more rigorous in the period we are discussing.

III. Examples of core societies include Spain and Portugal in the initial phases of the early modern period and Britain, France, and Holland by the 17th century.

    A. A core society makes profits from the world economy by exporting finished goods, organizing the trading companies that direct world commerce, and building and running the ships that carry trade. In the long term, the core society profits from the world economy because of its capacity to control activities and facilities in these three categories.

    B. Economic advantage, however, is closely linked to political advantage. In Wallerstein's view, core societies not only have profitable economic relationships internationally, but they also have fairly strong states.

        1. As a society profits from the international economy, tax revenues increase, enabling the society to fund a more elaborate system of government.

        2. With a strong government backed by a strong military, a core society can intervene in international situations in ways that will help position its merchants advantageously.

    C. Wallerstein also argues that core societies increasingly adopt wage labor systems, using wages to motivate workers and to locate workers where manufacturing opportunities exist.

IV. Peripheral societies are the mirror image of core societies.

    A. Peripheral societies have dependent economies through which they import expensive products primarily from core societies and export raw, unprocessed goods.

    B. Trade in peripheral societies is carried by merchants from core societies and depends heavily on ships from core economies.

C. Obviously, peripheral societies tend to lose money in international economic exchange. They are just as fully engaged in trade as core societies, but their engagement involves systematic disadvantages.

D. Peripheral societies have weak governments because they do not have the tax revenues to strengthen government. The core societies have a stake in keeping these governments weak so that their own merchants and interventions will not encounter resistance.

E. Peripheral economies (at least in the early modern period) do not rely primarily on wage labor but on forced or coercive labor, slavery, or harsh serfdom.

V. These economic, political, and social system or labor system relationships are easily uncovered in the early modern period.

    A. The core societies initially were Spain and Portugal, although ultimately, their positions slipped. In the end, the great core societies were those in much of the European northwest—France, Holland, Britain, and others.

        1. These societies spawned large trading companies that organized trade and sent out ships.

        2. These societies also experienced a significant and steady increase in manufacturing, including both craft manufacturing and domestic or home production.

    B. In using Wallerstein's theory, we need to guard against oversimplification.

        1. For example, although France and Britain were both core societies, France had a much stronger government and military than Britain in the early modern period.

    C. The classic peripheral society, of course, was Latin America.

        1. Latin America produced sugar, silver, wood products, and other goods that were mostly sent elsewhere for processing.

        2. In its colonial period, Latin America experienced quite weak governments.

        3. Latin American economies featured, essentially, versions of serfdom, the *encomienda* and *hacienda* systems, in which laborers were forced either to work certain days or to turn over certain percentages of their products.

D. Wallerstein notes that by the 18th century, peripheries were developing in parts of Eastern Europe, particularly Poland; there, amid harsh serfdom conditions, emphasis was increasingly placed on producing grain for sale in Western markets. In this trade, we see Polish reliance on the export of relatively cheap products, carried in Western ships, in patterns organized by Western merchant companies.

E. West Africa can also be seen as a peripheral economy if we argue that slaves constitute unprocessed goods.

    1. African slave systems developed through a combination of African merchant and political organization, occasionally with some direct European intervention. Slaves were then sold to European traders and transported by European ships and commercial companies.

    2. In return, African merchants and political figures received processed goods from the core societies.

VI. In looking at the peripheral societies, again, we need to be aware of oversimplification and some other rough points in categorization.

A. For example, although West Africa was a peripheral society, its governments were much stronger than those of Latin America and much more capable of regulating European activity.

B. As European intervention increased in India and what is now Indonesia, economies there developed some peripheral characteristics, although they did not shift entirely to a peripheral status.

C. The British colonies in North America also present problems of categorization.

    1. The South, with its concentration on the production of sugar and other goods for sale to Europe, clearly was a periphery.

    2. The middle colonies and New England, however, did not fit easily into Wallerstein's scheme. These areas had a significant local merchant class, engaged in some manufacturing, and ran some shipping, but they were not yet core economies.

VII. The key issue in Wallerstein's theory, however, is Asia.

    A. Wallerstein does not deal with Asia in great detail in his treatment of the early modern period, but the implications of his work suggest that Asia must be viewed largely as an external economy, that is, the Asian economy was not sufficiently involved in world trade to be affected by world trade dimensions.

        1. This position feeds and is fed by misperceptions about Asia's economic role in the world in this period, including its degree of isolation and disdain for commerce.

        2. If we dispel these notions, the idea of externality must be largely dispelled as well.

    B. Japan had the one clear external Asian economy by the 17th century.

        1. Around 1600, the Japanese cut off elaborate contacts with the West; without question, Japan's economy was not a significant participant in world trade patterns in the 17th and 18th centuries.

        2. Because Japan recognized the utility of maintaining some outlet to the wider world, however, the Japanese allowed the Dutch to trade near the port of Nagasaki.

        3. Externality was not complete, but Japan fits the external category fairly well in this period. Indeed, the early modern period saw considerable development of commercial operations in Japan, although not as a result of external economic relations.

    C. For the Middle East, India, and particularly China, however, externality simply does not apply.

        1. China received the largest amount of New World silver of any society in the 16th–18th centuries, largely as the European solution to its old balance-of-payments problem for Chinese exports.

        2. This flood of silver into China had significant impact. In the 17th century, for example, the Chinese government decided that all taxes must be paid in silver currency.

This requirement almost certainly resulted in increased inequality for peasants.

   3. China could not possibly earn this much New World silver and be regarded as an external economy, but it is not exactly core either because Chinese merchants and ships did not go out into the world beyond Southeast Asia.

   4. China was a manufacturing powerhouse but not, for foreign trade purposes, a commercial powerhouse; China had a strong government and traded actively with Southeast Asia, but on a global basis it did not operate as a core society.

D. Some of the same points apply to India, at least until the 18th century.

   1. India was the second largest recipient of New World silver because the Indians also had a variety of goods that Europeans desired. India, however, had little need for European goods during the early modern period.

   2. By the 18th century, with increased foreign intervention in India, its position shifted into a more dependent category, but for most of the early modern period both India and the Middle East had some advantage in trade with Europeans.

VIII. A modified view of the early modern world economy system makes sense.

A. With regard to Latin America, Africa, and some parts of Eastern Europe, European economic dominance is real; it is a source of new profits for the West and new patterns of economic and political activity for the peripheral societies.

B. Nonetheless, this is not yet a world system, and it must be modified to account for not only the decline of Spain and Portugal but the new position of India. Wallerstein's picture is further complicated by such factors as population shortages and cultural attitudes.

C. Properly adjusted, Wallerstein's theory explains why different societies fell into systematic patterns of inequality in the international marketplace in the early modern period and why this system tended to be so persistent. It is possible to fall out of the core, as Spain and Portugal did, but it is much more difficult to climb out of the periphery.

Further Reading:

Immanuel Wallerstein, *The Modern World-System II: Mercantilism and the Consolidation of the European World-Economy, 1600–1750.*

Kenneth Pomeranz, *The Great Divergence: China, Europe, and the Making of the Modern World Economy.*

David Eltis, et al., eds., *Slavery in the Development of the Americas.*

Questions to Consider:

1. Why and in what ways was much of Asia long resistant to the core/periphery relationships in the world economy?

2. Do the core and periphery models adequately capture relationships among economic, political, and social forms during the early modern period?

Lecture Twenty—Transcript
The World Economy, 1450–1750

In introducing the early modern period of world history in our last session, I emphasized—I frankly think it's pretty obvious—that the big deal development underlying all the others was the intensification of world economic relationships and the inclusion of the Americas into those relationships. What we're talking about today fleshes this basic statement out, adds detail, and adds theoretical rigor as we talk about the emergence of a new kind of world economy. Again, obviously, the Americas are included. The intensification point is really vital. When we talked about the world network in the postclassical period, we mentioned, for example, that by the time of the Song dynasty in China, the world network was really capable of having an impact on basic manufacturing patterns, increasing China's stake in the industrial sector, making silk, porcelain, etc.

When we talk about the early modern period, we're talking about the same kind of intensification operating in a whole set of different economies and operating at a higher level. The device we'll use to explore these points is, again, called *world economy theory*. It's the child of an American sociologist, Immanuel Wallerstein, who has a number of books on the subject—fairly thick, fairly intriguing, and fairly controversial. I find world economy theory—which is not absolutely brand new; it utilizes some Marxists perceptions and it utilizes economic work on dependency theory—a really useful device to talk about relationships in the early modern period and relationships that would endure even beyond, even to the present day.

The theory has, in my judgment, three advantages, in addition to illustrating the general points about intensification. First of all, it clarifies new systematic inequalities in international economic relationships that begin to emerge in the early modern period. Through this, it helps show why societies otherwise as different as Latin America and Poland actually can be viewed through something of the same lens. Second, it talks about relationships within societies between export and import activities, economic position in the world economy, and political structures and labor systems. These relationships are really interestingly interconnected, and I think the interconnections are, in many cases, plausible. The third advantage—

which obviously we will evoke today but have to come back to—is world economy's utility in helping to explain why certain kinds of patterns internationally endure so long, how hard they are to get rid of.

The theory has been, however, widely criticized, and we have to note this, too. Indeed, I think exploring the criticisms helps make the theory more useful. It's a theory that leaves out some factors. We will note in the following discussion that Wallerstein has almost no place for culture. I think culture is very important, even in the early modern world economy. I would try to add cultural factors in. There's surprisingly little attention [paid], actually, to explicit technologies. I think these can be added in without too much difficulty. There are certain omissions. Almost inevitably, there are oversimplifications. We'll point out some of these, as well. Wallerstein is generalizing about a wide array of territories and situations, and his model sometimes just shades off from necessary detail. This is not too hard to fix, but we need to work on fixing it. The theory has trouble dealing with change. That is, perhaps, one of the most telling deficiencies. It's very easy, using the theory, to say that society x is in this position at this time. But when society x changes from this position to that position, all the theory can do is say, "Gee, it shifted; we need to use the next category." It doesn't deal with change or explain change too clearly. Finally—also extremely important for the early modern period—the theory does not do justice to the complexity of patterns in Asia. Indeed, it may really distort. This has been the most recent attack, and we need to build this criticism in.

We're presenting a theory. I think it's useful for this period and the next and even into our own day. It has flaws. It can be amended. Let's get going. Wallerstein introduces three key concepts. He actually has four, but I'm going to simplify the simplification just a little bit. First of all, he talks about core societies. These are societies that are the winners in the early modern world economy. I'll explain their specific characteristics a bit more in a moment. Second, he talks about peripheral societies. These are the losers. Again, they have several characteristics that attach to their dependent, weaker position. Third, because not all societies were fully enmeshed in the world economy at this point, he also talks about external societies, where prosperity may or not exist, but where it's not primarily dependent on global economic relationships. We'll need this category, as well, although we also need to adjust Wallerstein's use of it.

There is one other preliminary. Wallerstein argues that these economic relationships—particularly core-periphery, which is the crucial duo—are born with the early modern period. We can see that elements of these relationships existed even in the postclassical period. It was not as rigorous because the intensity of the linkages wasn't as great, but there were societies that benefited more from exchange than others did—for example, China or the Middle East. There were also societies that tended to produce cruder products in their efforts to get into the game—for example, Western Europe. The relationships are not brand new, but we can start with the early modern because they certainly become more rigorous at this point.

Here's what a core society is: a society such as Spain or Portugal in the initial phases in the early modern period; a society such as Britain, France, or Holland, by the 17th century. A core society makes profits from the world economy by doing three things simultaneously. First, it exports finished goods, because you can make more money with finished goods because you have to pay for more stages of the production process than with less finished goods. It's an exporter of, largely, manufactured products. Second, it organizes the trading companies in which world commerce is carried. It makes money not just from manufacturing but also from commercial transactions. Third, it builds the ships and runs the ships that carry the trade, as well—another source of profit. Of course, there's risk in all these levels, as well. Sea trade in the early modern period was frequently beset by accidents, piracy, etc., so profit wasn't assured, but in the long term, the core profits from the world economy [arose] because of its [the core society's] capacity to operate superior activities and facilities in these three categories.

Economic advantage is, however, closely linked to political advantage. Here, Wallerstein isn't always clear as to which comes first. Probably, actually in his view, the politics comes first. In Wallerstein's view, core societies not only have profitable economic relationships internationally, [but] they also have fairly strong states. The connection is quite clear. In the first place, if you're profiting from the international economy, your tax revenues go up, so you can afford a more elaborate system of government. Second, if you have a strong government, backed by a strong military, you can intervene in international situations in ways that will help position your merchants advantageously. There is advantageous economic position coupled with political strength. Third, Wallerstein argues that core societies—and he's certainly empirically correct for the early modern period—will increasingly adopt wage labor systems because they need the capacity to use wages to motivate workers and to move them around where manufacturing opportunities exist. Other systems of labor simply won't work as well. Again, as a matter of fact, there's no question that wage labor spread in the early modern period. Whether it's quite so inherently attached to Wallerstein's system, one could debate.

Peripheral societies are the mirror image of core. They have dependent economies through which they will import expensive stuff from the core, primarily. They will export cheap stuff—raw, unprocessed goods of one sort or another. The trade will be carried by merchants from the core, so peripheral societies have a fairly small merchant class, mainly engaged in local exchanges—not nonexistent but small. Peripheral societies will depend heavily on the ships from the core economies, as well. They will obviously tend to lose money in international economic exchange. They're just as fully engaged in it as the core, but they're engaged at a series of systematic disadvantages. Peripheral societies will also have weak governments. Their governments will be weak because, again, they don't have the tax revenues to do much better. They're also weak because the core will want to keep them weak, so that its merchants and its interventions will not encounter significant political resistance.

Peripheral economies, finally, will rely not primarily on wage labor—at least in the early modern period—but on forced or coercive labor, slavery or harsh serfdom. Wallerstein isn't necessarily entirely clear as to why this is so. The argument obviously would be that because you're producing cheap products, you need cheap labor. But I think we can add one ingredient here that helps explain the situation more fully. Remember that in the early modern period, many peripheral societies also faced a labor shortage because of the dying off of native populations. If it relied on wage labor, the wages would tend to be fairly high because of supply and demand. The effort was, instead, to introduce slavery or some sort of serfdom in order to cut those costs that would result from a market economy operating on its own. Coercive labor was an extensive form.

These relationships—and, again, we're talking about economic, political, and social system or labor system relationships—are clearly easily uncovered in the early modern period. Again, the great core societies were initially Spain and Portugal. Then, their positions slipped as they failed to capitalize on their economic advantages and passed increasing manufacturing and trade opportunities northward in Europe. Ultimately, the great core societies were the societies of much of the European northwest—France, Holland, Britain, and some other participants to a lesser degree. These were the societies that ultimately generated the great trading companies—British, Dutch, East India Companies, etc.—that clearly organized the trade and sent the ships. Also, these were the societies that experienced a significant and steady increase of manufacturing. This includes both craft manufacturing—pouring artistic goods into the world economy—and also domestic or home production. Domestic manufacturing was where mostly rural workers would combine some agriculture with [such] work [as] making thread, cloth, simple metal equipment, nails, and that sort of thing. The core societies, as you actually look at them, clearly illustrate the increasing realization that money was to be made by organizing the trade very deliberately and increasingly realizing that money was to be made by emphasizing new levels of manufacturing.

Again, we do need, as I mentioned earlier, to guard against oversimplification. France and Britain, both core societies, were clearly not the same society in the early modern period. France is a classic illustration of Wallerstein's claim that core societies will have strong governments with strong militaries. The British government wasn't feeble, but this was, of course, a period in which Britain underwent considerable political turmoil and emerged with a relatively small government and, periodically, a fairly weak military, though always a strong navy. In other words, Wallerstein's basic claims about the core probably worked, but we need to be aware that we need to make some internal distinctions, as well.

The classic periphery, of course, was Latin America. Latin America produced sugar, produced silver, produced wood products, and produced other goods that were not processed there for the most part but sent elsewhere. Latin America did, in its colonial period, experience quite weak governments. They were weak not only because of core intervention, but also because the landlords and mine owners in the Latin American economy wanted to be free from government regulation as they worked to exploit their coercive labor. Certainly, Latin America developed coercive labor systems. The importation of slaves—particularly to the Caribbean and Brazil—for work in sugar plantations was a classic case in point. But in other areas also, with regard to native or Mestizo populations, Latin American economies featured, essentially, versions of serfdom, where labor would be partly coerced, partly forced, either to work certain days for the mine or the estate owner or to turn over certain percentages of produce—systems such as the *encomienda* and the *hacienda* system. They're not called serfdom in Latin American history, but if we step back a bit, they have very similar overtones.

Peripheries could develop elsewhere. Wallerstein notes that by the 18th century, peripheries were developing in parts of Eastern Europe, particularly Poland, where amid another set of harsh serfdom conditions, emphasis increasingly went to producing grain for sale in Western markets. As Britain particularly converted increasingly to manufacturing, it would need to import food from other places. They sought this food at low prices. Poland and other parts of Eastern Europe were willing to oblige. And, again, [these societies had] weak government. The Polish government was notoriously weak in the early 18th century. There were harsh labor conditions, serfdom, and reliance on the export of relatively cheap products, carried in Western ships, in patterns organized by Western merchant companies, etc.

Africa, West Africa particularly, can also be seen as a peripheral economy if we take the step of arguing that slaves constitute something of an unprocessed good. African slave systems obviously developed through a combination of African merchants and political organizations seeking the slaves and bringing them to the coast, occasionally with some direct European intervention, and then selling them to European slave traders on the coast. The goods were relatively unprocessed. The ships and the commercial companies were European. In return, African merchants and political figures received processed goods, again, from the core.

The key goods were, again, slaves, sugar, silver, and wood products. A bit later, cotton would be added to the mix. The core products that went into the world economy were, particularly, guns—of great interest, for example, to African political leaders. Also, there was an increasing array of European craft products—tapestries, paintings, fancy furniture, and that sort of thing—which could adorn the homes of the successful members of the peripheral economies. Peripheral economies, it should be added, were poor, but there could be some very rich people who made money from the agricultural estates and the mines. Mostly, these people would not put their money back into the local economy, but money there was.

Here, too, with the periphery, we need to note some oversimplifications. If West Africa was a periphery, we have to note that its governments were much stronger than those of Latin America, much more capable of regulating European activity. The specifics of the pattern are distinct, and again, we need to guard against Wallersteinian oversimplification.

Other societies began to demonstrate at least a few peripheral characteristics by the 18th century. Particularly as European intervention increased in India and what is now Indonesia, economies were increasingly turned to production of goods, such as spices, teas, etc. The economy as a whole was not yet shifted to peripheral status, but some peripheral characteristics were developing. Again, Wallerstein can't explain changes of this sort— you have to look at military and political intervention, the use of military technology—but he can pick up the category once it begins to emerge.

There are some rough spots quite apart from the oversimplification. What does one do, for example, with the British colonies of North America? The South, clearly, was a periphery. As Southerners concentrated on the production of sugar and other goods for sale to Europe, they fall quite clearly into a peripheral category. Later on, they would actually be a periphery of the American North, particularly as cotton production spread. But for the middle colonies, particularly, and for New England, it's not quite so easy to figure out where to put them in the Wallersteinian scheme. These areas had a significant local merchant class. They did some manufacturing. They ran some shipping. They're not yet core—i.e., they're certainly dependent on European monitoring—but it's not just an easy category. We just have to recognize that not every size fits all in this theoretical discussion.

The key issue, however, as I mentioned before, is Asia. Wallerstein doesn't necessarily talk in great detail about Asia in his treatment of the early modern period, but the implications of his work would suggest that Asia must be viewed largely through the lens of externality. That is, the Asian economy is not sufficiently involved in world trade to be affected by world trade dimensions one way or another. This position, which feeds and is fed by real misperceptions about Asia's economic role in the world at this point—by misperceptions about degrees of isolation, degrees of disdain for commerce, all the old stereotypes, particularly applied to China but sometimes more widely, as well—these perceptions have to be dispelled in order to understand the key point. With this, the notion of externality has to be largely dispelled, as well.

There was one clear external Asian economy by the 17th century, and that was the economy of Japan. The Japanese decision substantially to isolate, taken around 1600, to cut off elaborate contacts with the West, included new regulations against Japanese trade with other societies, new regulations against foreigners working in Japan, and without question, Japan's economy was not a significant participant in world trade patterns in the 17th and 18th centuries. There was still a chink open. The Japanese allowed the Dutch to trade near the port of Nagasaki because they recognized that having some outlet to the wider world might still be useful. The Dutch, at this point, did not seem particularly menacing, for example, compared to the Catholic Spaniards. Externality was not complete, but an external category would actually work pretty well for Japan in this period. It was consistent with considerable internal commercial growth. The early modern period sees significant development of commercial operations in Japan—new companies processing foods, making beer, this sort of thing. This was a fairly dynamic period in the Japanese economy, but not because of external economic relations of any major sort.

But for China, the Middle East, and India—particularly for China—externality simply doesn't work. Here's probably the favorite world history fact, currently. I mention it to you so you can impress your friends. What society received the largest amount of New World silver in the 16th, 17th, and 18th centuries? The intuitive answer would probably be Spain, or maybe if you recognize that Spain's position eroded after a while, maybe Britain or France. The actual answer, very definitely, is China. China got more silver from the New World than any other society, and the reason is very simple. Remember [that] the old dilemma that we tend to forget by the early modern period still operates. Europeans had long sought Chinese goods. They still sought Chinese goods. It's in the 17th century, for example, that the word *china* enters the English language to mean "porcelain." They really wanted this stuff. They still have nothing that they can use to pay for it. In a famous passage at the end of the 18th century, a British envoy to the Qing emperor of China prostrates himself, as one is supposed to do in the presence of this august figure, but urges that the Chinese open their markets to the British. He carries a letter from the British monarch urging this opening and the Chinese emperor is very vigorous in reply: "Thank you very much, but there's nothing from the outside world that we need. Why don't you go home?" The Chinese simply did not need European goods. They produced better goods themselves, or they didn't want them, as in the case of massive supplies of guns. What were the Europeans to do? In the early modern period—the dilemma is an old one, we've seen it in the postclassical period—in the early modern period, there is a new European answer: "Hooray, we now have silver from the New World, and we'll send this to the Chinese." This is where the Europeans appear not just as dynamic economic entrepreneurs and manufacturers, though they have this role in certain areas, but as transmitters. They're simply taking a valued American good as carriers to the Chinese and getting what they want in return.

Silver flooded China with significant impact. In the 17th century, the Chinese government decides, for example, that all taxes must now be paid in silver currency. It was a huge challenge to many ordinary peasants who had to increase their market activities in order to try to earn the silver they would have to use for taxation purposes. Social inequality almost certainly increased in China. There's a lot of adverse criticism by Chinese observers about this monetization and commercialization of the Chinese society. The point is not just that China is making a lot of profit from this system, but that it's a profit level that will affect Chinese society in other ways, as well. The point for world economy theory is, clearly, [that] China is an active participant, but it doesn't quite fit any of the models that Wallerstein has put forward. It's not external. You couldn't possibly earn this much New World silver and be regarded as external. You are involved in world trade; you are impacted by world trade. But it's not exactly core either, although that might be the closest fit. It's not core because Chinese merchants and ships are not going out into the world as a whole. China is a production powerhouse, and many Chinese today, as China's manufacturing position again becomes central to global trade, argue that China is quite simply restoring what it had once achieved after a brief and troubled interruption—an interesting vantage point that we will return to. China was a manufacturing powerhouse. It was not, for foreign trade purposes, a commercial powerhouse. It did trade actively still with Southeast Asia. Again, we want to dispel any notion that the Chinese are just sitting there letting Westerners bring stuff to them or that the Chinese are somehow disinclined to trade. On a global basis, the Chinese clearly are not operating the way a core society is supposed to. They have a strong government. They might fit a core definition in other respects, but the category just has to be adjusted. This is a different situation.

Some of the same comments apply to India, at least until the 18th century. India is the second largest recipient of New World silver because the Indians also have a variety of goods that Europeans want. They have fine cotton and other kinds of cloth. They have spices. They have a mixture, in other words, of specialized agricultural products and manufactured products. Again, they have very little need for European goods during the early modern period. New World silver is, once more, the grease that operates this particular commercial machine. As we've noted, by the 18th century, when foreign intervention increases in India, this enviable position may begin to shift into a clearer dependent category, but for most of the early modern period, India and the Middle East, as well, trade with some advantage with Europeans. They're not dominated by Europeans, but they're not removed from international trade either. You simply need—for the early modern period, at least—a separate Asian category that would then allow for specific cases, such as Japan.

I think it's pretty clear—though, again, argument is welcome—that a modified early modern world economy system makes considerable sense. With regard to Latin America, to some extent Africa, and increasingly, some parts of Eastern Europe, European economic dominance is very real. It's a source of new profits for the West; it's a source of new patterns of economic and political activity for the peripheral societies involved. This is not yet a world system. It does not yet embrace most of Asia. It needs to be modified to take changes into account—not only the economic decline of Spain and Portugal but the new position of India. We'll talk about some relevant changes for Russia in a later comment, as well. We need to add to Wallerstein a sense of change. We need to recognize that his picture must be complicated by factors, such as population shortage, cultural attitudes, etc. We need to make a great big adjustment for many key parts of Asia as against not only his tendency but also the larger stereotypes that are simply, simply wrong for this period. But with these adjustments, I think we come back to the three key points that I suggested at the outset.

Properly adjusted, Wallerstein does explain why different societies fell into some systematic patterns of inequality in the international marketplace in the early modern period. He does explain why weak government has some relationship to dependent economic status. Above all—though here we can only make a statement at this point, and we'll come back to it as we move on in time—he does explain why this system tended to be so persistent. It is possible to fall out of the core—Spain and Portugal did—if you don't make full use of your economic superiority, but it's hard, because you make enough money from this system that you can make some mistakes and still be on top. It's even harder, probably, to climb out of the periphery. If you're not making money from the world economic system, if your labor force is abused and impoverished, if your merchant class is small, it's going to be very difficult to change this position. It's not impossible, because we will see later on that people do, societies do emerge, but persistence—the connections between early modern economic relationships and even contemporary economic issues in the world economy; this connection is vivid—but this demonstrates the persistence of the kinds of categories Wallerstein establishes.

Lecture Twenty-One
Transformations in Western Europe

Scope:

Partly because of its growing world role and rising earnings from international trade, Western Europe changed greatly in the three centuries after 1450. Many of the items on a list of key developments are quite familiar: the Renaissance, including the Northern Renaissance; the Protestant and Catholic Reformations; the price revolution of the 16th century (prompted by the import of increasing amounts of silver and promoting further commercial expansion); the rise of absolutism (but also the advent of parliamentary monarchies in Britain and Holland); the Scientific Revolution; and the Enlightenment. These developments did not all neatly mesh, and other interesting episodes suggested some of the tensions involved with uneven and sometimes contradictory change—the witchcraft craze of the 17th century is a leading case in point. From a world history standpoint, there are two major issues: First, with all due credit to the growing importance of the West, it would be misleading to linger too long over the details of activities in a single society. Second, these changes must be placed in a world history context—compared with developments elsewhere and assessed for their greater impact. The focus of this lecture, then, is on the big changes in the West and their larger implications for world history. This focus, in turn, calls for attention to growing commercialization in the economy, which paralleled the larger international role; the growth of state functions and the emergence of the nation state; and a series of changes in both formal and popular culture, many of them revolving around the rise of science.

Outline

I. The early modern centuries constituted an exceptionally busy time for Western Europe.

   A. The list of major European activities during this time is formidable:

      1. The migration of the Renaissance to the north from about 1450 onward.

      2. The 16th-century Protestant and Catholic Reformations.

3. The price revolution.

4 The rise of absolutism in the 17th century.

5. The parliamentary monarchies that developed in Britain and the Netherlands.

6. The Scientific Revolution.

7. The 18th-century Enlightenment.

B. World history does not afford us the opportunity to spend as much time on these developments as we might in a Western civilization approach. How can we make this range of developments in Western Europe manageable enough to fit into a world history pattern?

C. In this lecture, we will take "a big changes approach," looking at significant shifts in Western Europe between 1450 and 1750. This approach does not do justice to all the individual movements and currents in Western Europe but is necessary for understanding the bigger picture.

D. We will also look briefly at the global implications of these changes.

E. We will evaluate the big changes in the West in terms of their placement among existing global standards.

II. Big changes in the West in the early modern period fall into four categories.

A. First is the increasing place of the West in world trade and, to a lesser extent, in world power politics. From world trade, the West gained access to new ideas and perspectives and new levels of wealth and commercial opportunity. Although we will focus on the other three big developments in the West, this repositioning in the world was a fundamental change in and of itself.

B. The other three big developments involved an increasing commercialization of the West European economy, increasing governmental efficiency and rationalization, and fundamental shifts in cultural outlook.

III. The first of the three is commercialization.

    A. During the 16th, 17th, and 18th centuries, more Europeans became involved in the commercial economy, producing at least some goods for sale on the market.

        1. In the 17th century, southern French peasants and landlords began producing wine for sale to other regions, thus involving themselves in importing food for consumption.

        2. Villages began to specialize in certain kinds of production. In both agriculture and manufacturing, ordinary people, as well as merchants and landlords, began to produce more for the market and to adopt an explicit set of market motivations and practices.

        3. This meant a growing importance for the merchant class of Western Europe, which expanded and gained wealth from both international and domestic trade.

        4. The expansion of domestic manufacturing in Western Europe was also important. Under this system, rural people devoted more effort to producing goods for sale to merchants in nearby cities.

    B. Commercialization was accompanied by a growing gap between the large numbers of people who owned property and the propertyless or near propertyless workers.

        1. European class structure shifted away from the community-based relationships that had predominated in the postclassical centuries.

        2. This change was accompanied by a new and harsher attitude toward poverty, even as early as the late-16th century.

    C. This commercialization of the European economy falls under the heading of a catch-up development. It brought Europe to economic levels that had previously been achieved in such places as China and other parts of Asia.

    D. By the 18th century, developments began to press beyond the catch-up level.

        1. The expansion of domestic manufacturing and the introduction of new technologies (such as the flying shuttle in weaving) pushed the European economy beyond levels that had been achieved in other societies.

2. Another 18th-century development — recently uncovered — is the beginning of modern consumerism in Western Europe, predating the Industrial Revolution.

IV. The second category of development is politics.

A. Until the 17th century, European politics can still broadly be described in terms of the earlier emphasis on feudalism. But by the 17th century, though feudal remnants lingered, European states were beginning to develop a new range of activities and a sense of rationalization.

B. Central governments now began to send out increasing numbers of bureaucrats to the provinces to ensure that central edicts were enforced uniformly throughout the realm and to monitor local conditions. At this point, national boundaries began to matter.

C. New functions included such activities as cultural intervention. In the 17th century, the French monarchy, for example, established an institution to monitor and regularize the French language; and in this same period, European states began to set up prisons.

D. Along with the expansion of function came rationalization, an increasingly self-conscious effort to think through how government activities were organized. The military serves as a prime example: in the 17th century, many European armies began to acquire uniforms, define officer grades, formalize training for officers, organize hospitals and logistical systems, and establish pensions.

E. Most of these developments were catch-up activities, that is, European governments were now beginning to do things that political systems in several other societies had already done, although, again, with particular European emphases.

F. By the 17th and 18th centuries, however, we see an innovative twist—the clear beginnings of the idea of a nation state, a state in which a shared culture and tradition would coexist with the state itself. The nation state concept was a fundamental innovation on the world scene that would have a wide impact beyond Europe as well as within it.

V. The third category of development is culture.

   A. The advent of printing in Europe opened up massive opportunities for Europeans to have contact with the written word. Literacy advanced systematically, and by the 18th century Western Europe had the highest literacy rates of any large society in the world.

   B. The Protestant Reformation, despite some effective Catholic response, shattered the unity of Western Christianity and led to internal conflicts and tensions. In the long run it tended to reduce religious commitment in Europe and promote some idea of religious toleration.

   C. During the Scientific Revolution of the 17th century, the range of scientific discovery and the increasing sense on the part of many intellectuals that the key to truth lay in science (not faith or tradition) was a fundamental change that no other scientific endeavor in other societies matched.

   D. If we combine science with printing and growing literacy rates, we could argue that of the three areas we have emphasized—commercialization, political change, and culture—it is culture that makes Western Europe stand out from other societies.

   E. The other intriguing aspect of cultural change in early modern Europe was the degree to which it penetrated into relatively prosaic activities and into the attitudes of relatively ordinary people. Between about 1600 and 1700, people had vastly different responses to ordinary situations, such as losing a valued object, naming a child, or embarking on marriage.

   F. Fundamental shifts in Western culture yielded impressive and varied expressions at the level of popular beliefs and practices, affecting the sense of the individual, the sense of family and community, and attitudes toward risk and nature.

VI. Western Europe, despite all the exciting things happening there, was not the only place in the world.

   A. Many regions continued to ignore developments in the West, and some areas, by coincidence, saw a few developments that were not unlike those occurring in the West.

B. Nonetheless, the changes that occurred in the West in the early modern centuries have three final implications.

   1. The big changes we have seen—governments taking on new roles, new attitudes toward nature, and even new attitudes toward children—almost guaranteed that additional changes would occur in the West. Of course, the increasing pace of commercialization set the fundamental framework here.

   2. These changes would color European reactions to other societies. Europeans would think of other places as uncivilized because they did not measure up to Europe's new standards.

   3. The developments that occurred in the West set a challenging target for other societies. The complexity of the Western model would affect responses to Western activities in the wider world as well.

Further Reading:

Charles Tilly, *Big Structures, Large Processes, Huge Comparisons.*

Robert Dear, *Revolutionizing the Sciences: European Knowledge and Its Ambitions, 1500–1700.*

Ulinka Rublack, *Reformation Europe.*

Mary Hartman, *The Household and the Making of History: A Subversive View of the Western Past.*

Questions to Consider:

1. How did religious change in Western Europe, notably the rise of Protestantism and the Catholic response, help explain the longer-term changes in commerce, politics, and popular culture?

2. Compared to other major agricultural civilizations by the 18th century, such as China or the Middle East, what was unusual and what was fairly standard about Western institutions and culture?

Lecture Twenty-One—Transcript
Transformations in Western Europe

It's no secret that the early modern centuries constituted an exceptionally busy time for Western Europe—many changes and significant movements. We'll be dealing with basic shifts in our discussion today, but we need to begin with a slight sense of caution and, certainly, a concern with making sure the developments we'll be discussing fit into a world history context.

The list of major European activities is formidable. You start with the Renaissance. The Italian Renaissance began before 1450, of course, but 1450 itself is the conventional date at which one notes the migration of the Renaissance to the north. The 16th century saw the Protestant Reformation, the Catholic Reformation in response, and the price or commercial revolution that was stimulated by the advent of precious metals from the New World and which encouraged additional commercial activity in Europe. The 17th century sees the rise of absolutism, the variant that developed in Britain and the Netherlands with the emergence of a new modern form of parliamentary monarchy. Of course, it saw the Scientific Revolution, one of the incontestably great developments of the early modern period. The 18th century sees, above all, the Enlightenment, a popularization and expansion of scientific thinking. It also sees the application of some Enlightenment ideas to absolute monarchy in the form of enlightened despotism. The list is obviously considerable and it's important.

The issue for starters is how we make sure that this range of developments in Western Europe becomes manageable enough to fit into a world history pattern. Let me illustrate by raising a specific question, which I won't exactly answer, though I'm going to imply my reaction. How much, from the standpoint of world history, do we need to know about the European Renaissance? Here's one of the great staples, the glorious staples, of the tradition of Western civilization, lovingly detailed, particularly by people interested in artistic and cultural history. But from a world history standpoint, how much time can one afford to spend on the Renaissance? How much attention does it absolutely require? Here, I will answer from my own standpoint. My own reaction is, frankly, probably not much, but it can be debated. Certainly, world history does not afford the opportunity to spend as much time on the Renaissance, then the Reformation, then science, and then the Enlightenment as one would offer in a Western civilization approach. You just have to be more selective.

We're going to talk first about a "big changes" approach. That is, instead of going through Renaissance, Reformation, blah, blah, blah, we're going to be talking about what are the big ways that Western Europe shifted between 1450 and 1750. This does not do full justice to all of the individual movements and currents, which after all, were, among other things, not entirely consistent. The Renaissance, for example, had a more secular spirit; Reformation returns to a greater religious emphasis. These eddies are obviously extremely important if one has the luxury of a Western civilization framework, but they're not necessarily any more important than some of the countercurrents that one could also encounter in China, the Middle East, sub-Saharan Africa, etc. We have to look at the bigger picture. We'll be talking in the first instance about major categories of change, many of which, frankly, focus a bit more on the second half of the early modern period than on the first half, though of course, they're prepared by developments earlier on.

Two other controls are vital. In the first place, in addition to simplifying the usual picture so that it becomes appropriate for a world history framework, we will at the end talk more explicitly about [the question:] Okay, these things happened in the West; what are their global implications? This will be brief but, obviously, is also intended to make sure we don't get lost in the Western forest and lose sight of the bigger picture. I've mangled a metaphor there, but you know what I mean.

The final control within this discussion itself is, I think, a really interesting one. I venture it here a little bit cautiously, but I actually think it'll work. From a world history standpoint, what was going on in the West in the early modern period was partly playing catch-up. Remember, the West had been, by the top global standards, a somewhat backwards society during the postclassical period, though it changed a lot and it was beginning to move into a more global orbit by the end of the postclassical period. In the early modern period, the West does a number of things that bring it close to the levels already achieved in places such as China and the Middle East. Now, of course, it did so in specific ways that are Western. In broader outline—and I'll be able to point this out explicitly—we'll be able to see how the West adjusted, consciously or unconsciously, to existing global standards. The second angle involves attention to where the West actually innovated and did not follow basic patterns laid out already. We'll need to evaluate the big changes we'll be focusing on in terms of their placement, either as basically catch-up—with, again, perhaps a special Western twist—or as fundamentally innovative. I think this framework is actually quite interesting and appropriate. Of course, finally, we need to remember that what was going on in the West is matched by important developments in other parts of the world. We'll have a chance to come back to that in subsequent discussions.

The big changes in the West in the early modern period fall into four basic categories. One I will merely mention because we've already covered it, but in a way, it was the granddaddy of all categories, and that was the increasing place that the West was winning in world trade and, to a lesser extent, in world power politics. From world trade, the West gained access to new kinds of ideas and perspectives. It certainly gained access to new levels of wealth and commercial opportunity. Remember that, although we're now going to focus on the other three big developments, this repositioning in the world was a fundamental change in and of itself.

The other big developments involved an increasing commercialization of the West European economy, obviously pretty closely tied to global developments. There were significant changes in politics along the lines of increasing governmental efficiency and rationalization. Finally, there were significant, even fundamental, shifts in cultural outlook and in the way many Europeans began to think about the world. These developments occurred at the same time. They overlapped; they could reinforce each other. But I think it's useful, initially, to look at them one by one.

Let's look at commercialization. During the 16th, 17th, and 18th centuries, fairly steadily, more and more Europeans became involved in a commercial economy, producing at least some goods for sale on the market, for sale for money. This included farmers. For example, it was only in the 17th century that southern French peasants and landlords began producing wine for sale to other regions, thus involving themselves in importing other kinds of food they would need. Individual villages began to specialize in shoe production or nail production or scissors or cutlery production. Both in agriculture and in manufacturing, ordinary people, as well as merchants and landlords, began producing more for the market, began adopting an increasingly explicit set of market motivations and practices. The development was uneven. You could find a commercial village right next to a very traditional, self-sufficient one, but the general tendency was quite marked. This meant, of course, a growing importance for the merchant class of Western Europe, which expanded and gained wealth, both from international and from domestic trade. The expansion of a merchant and capitalist sector was an important part of this phenomenon. Absolutely crucial, as mentioned already in discussions of the world economy, was the expansion of domestic manufacturing in Western Europe. That system by which rural people, while still possibly doing some farming, devoted an increasing amount of their effort to producing goods for sale to merchants in nearby cities—goods such as textiles, particularly, of various sorts, but also, again, metal products, shoes, and potentially, other items. From the 16th through the 18th centuries, there was a steady expansion of European commercialization.

This had a couple of other corollaries. Most important, commercialization was accompanied by a growing gap between the large numbers of people who owned some property—an artisan shop, a bit of land, whatever—and an equally rapidly growing group of essentially propertyless or near propertyless workers, dependent on the sale of their labor for a wage. In other words, European class structure shifted away from the more community-based relationships that had predominated during the postclassical centuries. Along with this, in turn—and it's a striking development, even as early as the late 16th century—came a new and, frankly, harsher attitude toward poverty. Along with traditional religious views that the poor should receive charity, that they would always be with us, came an increasing sense that, frankly, if you were poor, there must be something wrong with you. Maybe not every poor person deserved assistance. This is an attitude that obviously still lingers in the Western psyche, although some other attitudes have joined in, as well.

The commercialization of the European economy—the expansion to domestic manufacturing, the increasing production of food products for sale on urban markets, etc.—in broad outline, [these] were catch-up developments. They brought Europe to economic levels that had previously been achieved in places such as China and other parts of Asia. They were not—again, aside from individual peculiarities—in and of themselves distinctive on the world scene. Attitudes toward poverty maybe had a little bit of additional edge. The witchcraft scare that was such an interesting sign of ongoing tension in European life in the 16th and 17th centuries had something to do with the new social framework that the Europeans were creating. A disproportionate number of accused witches were poor people, particularly poor women, feared among other things because of the new sense of hostility toward poverty. There are a few special twists, but in broad outline, this is a catch-up development.

By the 18th century, however—still on the theme of commercialization—developments began to press beyond a mere catch-up level in two senses. First, by this point, the expansion of domestic manufacturing and, now, the beginnings of new technologies—for example, the flying shuttle in the weaving of cloth, which was designed to increase the productivity of manual workers—these developments began to push the European economy beyond levels that had been achieved in other societies. It's still within range, but you're beginning to get a level of commercialization, attention to manufacturing and productivity levels that are on the verge, at least, of becoming distinctive.

The other 18th century development—and this is a striking, recent historical discovery—was the beginning of modern consumerism in Western Europe. We have noted at several earlier points that consumerism is hardly a purely modern phenomenon. Upper classes frequently indulged in a delight in material goods that they did not strictly need and a capacity to gain some sense of purpose and identity from consumer activities. But it's in the 17th, 18th centuries in Western Europe that consumerism begins to spread beneath the upper class and merchant level to more ordinary people—not everybody, of course—but to more ordinary people. It's at this point that consumer interests begin to take on the contours of some real passion. For example, in the 18th century, thefts of clothing accelerated massively, a sign that people were beginning to want things as part of their personal set of values and identities and would be willing to go beyond the law in order to obtain them. Again, they were things they did not, strictly speaking, need. This discovery that a modern form of consumerism predates the Industrial Revolution and is centered in Western Europe is indeed an important addition to our sense of what commercialization could accomplish—increasing commercial activity, largely in the catch-up mode but capable of pressing beyond that level to more genuine innovation on a world scale.

The second category of development is politics. Despite the rise of individual monarchs or the Renaissance city-states, until the 17th century, European politics can still broadly be described in terms of the earlier emphasis on feudalism. But by the 17th century, though feudal remnants lingered, European states—particularly in absolute monarchies such as that of France—were beginning to develop a new range of activities and sense of rationalization. Let me illustrate. First of all, a fairly familiar development, central governments now began to send out an increasing number of bureaucrats to the provinces to make sure that central edicts were enforced more uniformly throughout the realm, and local conditions, in turn, could be monitored by central authorities. It was at this point, for example, that national boundaries between countries such as France and Spain began really to matter, because it now mattered which state you belonged to.

New functions also included activities such as cultural intervention. It was in the 17th century that the French monarchy decided that it should set up an institution to help monitor and regularize the French language, an activity that the French state still conducts, perhaps in a more beleaguered fashion, in the present day. It was in this period also that European states began to set up prisons. It was a tremendous change in potential operations in criminal justice and a considerable expansion of the role of the state in dealing with criminals. The list is long.

Along with expansion of function, came this process we call rationalization, an increasingly self-conscious effort to think through how government activities were organized. The military serves as a prime example here. Again, it was in the 17th century that many European armies began to acquire set uniforms; that officer grades began to be systematically defined so there was a clear hierarchy of progression; that training for certain kinds of officers, particularly military engineers, began to be formalized; that new activities, such as hospitals and logistical systems for armies, began to be organized so that when an army moved through the countryside, it would not simply be living off the land; and even military pensions [were] established. European states became more active, conducting a wider array of functions, and their activities were increasingly rationalized.

Now in broad outline, most of this was catch-up. That is, European governments were now beginning to do things that political systems in several other societies—China obviously at the head—had done well before this. Again, particular European emphases—the prison system seems to have been unusually stressed in Europe, for example—but the broad patterns are familiar. There's no fundamental innovation. Europe gained increasingly the political capacity to operate on a global stage in tandem with the most advanced political systems in other societies. That's an important development, but it's not fundamentally novel. Here, too, particularly by the 17th and 18th centuries, [we see] a distinctive twist that was more innovative, and that is the clear beginnings of the idea of a nation-state. That is, a state in which a definition of shared culture and tradition would coexist with the state itself. This is a novel development. You might find hints of it in patterns that the Chinese had conducted earlier, but fundamentally, most states previously had not called on active loyalty of subjects to the extent that the nation-state did. They had not assumed that the state and the cultural orbit were coterminous. The nation-state concept, which would obviously develop still further in the later 18th and 19th centuries, was a fundamental innovation on the world scene, and it would have wide impact beyond Europe, as well as within it. Political changes are very significant, largely along fairly familiar lines if you use the standards of other societies, but with this particular new emphasis.

The third category is major developments in culture. Three fundamental shifts occurred, setting the framework for more detailed changes. In the first place, obviously, the establishment of printing in Europe, though initially devoted primarily to religious tracts, opened up massive expansions of opportunities for Europeans to have contact with the written word, to gain new sources of information, and this was a fundamental shift in the European cultural horizon. Literacy developed pretty systematically in the 16th, 17th, and 18th centuries. By the 18th century, Western Europe had the highest rates of literacy of any large society in the world. Other developments that followed from printing obviously included the emergence of newspapers, weekly for the most part, by the end of the 17th century. There's a new cultural apparatus here that's very significant.

Development number two: The Protestant Reformation, despite some effective Catholic response, shattered the unity of Western Christianity and led to all sorts of internal conflicts and tensions, but in the long run, it tended to reduce religious commitment in Europe and tended to increase an attachment to some idea of religious toleration. I know this simplifies a lot of very complicated developments, but I think that was the long-run impact.

Finally, the granddaddy of all three major cultural shifts was the Scientific Revolution itself. European science, as we've discussed previously, had, prior to this time, shared many features directly borrowed from many other scientific traditions, particularly those of the Middle East. But in the 17th century, the range of scientific discovery and the increasing sense on the part of many intellectuals—and even, through popularization, ordinary people— that the key to truth lay through science, not faith or tradition, this was a fundamental change that no other scientific endeavor in other societies had yet matched. European science, obviously, was not totally unique. We want to remember that vigorous scientific traditions existed in other societies, but the overall contours of the Scientific Revolution were really novel. Indeed, when you combine printing and growing literacy—the printing of materials directed at relatively ordinary people—when you combine this with science, one could argue that of all the three areas that we've been emphasizing— commercialization, political change, and culture—it's really culture that makes Western Europe increasingly stand out from the standards of other societies. This was not just an abstract development. The other intriguing aspect of cultural change in early modern Europe was how it penetrated into relatively prosaic activities and into the attitudes of relatively ordinary people. Let me offer a few illustrations from a fascinating array.

Illustration number one: If you lost a valued object in 1600, and you looked for it, you couldn't find it, but you really wanted to get it, you would normally employ a local "cunning man." This would be a magic person, who had a magic stick, and he would go around and shake the stick, and hopefully, the stick would help identify the lost object. Of course, if it didn't, you'd done the best you could. In 1720, take the same scenario—you lose something, you look for it, you really want it back, and you can't find it. You would no longer turn to the local cunning man because, increasingly, this person didn't exist. Instead, particularly if you lived in cities, you would do one of two things or both. You would advertise the lost object in the local newspaper or you would go to the city lost-and-found office, offices of the sort that were increasingly established from the later 17th century onward. It's a specific illustration of a broader phenomenon. During the 17th and 18th centuries, magical approaches to nature, magical approaches toward dealing with problems, such as lost-and-found [items], begin to pass from favor. Lots of people still believe in them. If you look at supermarket tabloids, lots of people still believe in them today, but they are no longer dominantly fashionable. Instead, people turned increasingly to a new kind of calculation of risk and a new kind of rational or scientific approach to nature, such that magical approaches now were either outright disapproved or relegated to obscure corners in some areas of popular life.

The second illustration is quite a different category. In 1650, if you had a child, you might wait to name it for about two years. When you did name it, you would probably choose either the name of a past relative, or the name of another child you had had who had died, or possibly a religious name. In 1750, when you had a child, you would normally name it now quickly. The child would still be likely to die, but the sense of the importance of dealing with the individual from birth was now on the upswing and that meant a new kind of naming practice. Second, when you did name the child, you would not normally pick a family name. You would never, never pick a name from a kid you'd had who'd already died. Indeed, you would often stay away from religious names. The new fashion was to look for new kinds of names that would express greater individuality and give a child a greater sense of being his or her own person.

Another category, and I'll end with this one, in a fascinating array: In 1650, if your father told you, a young girl, to get married and who to marry, you might protest individually, but you would almost certainly lose. Papa and maybe Mama would tell you who to marry, and the marriage would be arranged on the basis of family property considerations. In 1750, if Papa told you who to marry—you're still a young girl—and you felt you could not love that person, you might be able to persuade Papa that this was a match that should not occur because marriage had to be based upon affection. In a few places, such as some parts of Switzerland, if Papa didn't agree, you could actually go to court and get the arrangement cancelled. The notion that marriage should be based on love, should be a union that involved affection and even sexual expression and not just property arrangements, was born in this period. The list is long and the basic point, obviously, is clear.

Fundamental shifts in Western culture—science, religious division, growing literacy—yielded impressive and varied expressions at the level of popular beliefs and practices, affecting a sense of the individual, affecting a sense of family and community, and affecting, obviously, attitudes toward risk and nature. This is a big deal change and it marks the extent to which the cultural realm was probably particularly the area where the West was striking out in new directions.

Now, we come back to some cautions and final conclusions. Remember that Western Europe, despite all the exciting things happening there, was not the only place in the world. Lots of places continued to ignore what was going on in the West. Actually, some areas saw a few developments, by coincidence, that were not totally different than those occurring in the West. For example, in these same early modern centuries, many Confucian leaders in China began to attack popular superstition in magic in order to make Chinese life more rational and less dependent on folk superstition than had been the case. The West is not the only place where interesting developments were occurring, not the only place we want to look to as we get a sense of the early modern period as a whole.

But the changes that did occur in the West in the early modern centuries, when we take the big changes approach, have three final implications. Number one: They almost guaranteed that additional change would occur in the West itself. With governments taking on new roles, with new attitudes toward nature, even with new attitudes toward children—increasing interest in seeing children develop in a creative fashion—changes of this sort almost ensured that additional change was underway. Of course, the increasing pace of commercialization set the fundamental framework here.

Second, these changes would color European reactions to other societies. We've already noted that Europeans, as they moved into new positions in the world, often began to judge other societies by their technological level. Now, they might also begin to judge other societies by how much superstition seemed to be present and by how children were treated. It became increasingly easy for Europeans to think of other places as uncivilized because they didn't measure up to the new standards that were present in Europe itself. By the 19th century, for happily a fairly brief time, many Westerners in fact did decide that there were no traditions other than the Western that really merited the term *civilization* at all.

Finally, third, the developments that occurred in the West would set a challenging target for other societies as they looked at the West and increasing Western success and wondered what they might copy. For example, to take an obvious one, the European notion of the nation-state, the idea that the state and culture should coexist, proved to be very popular in other parts of the world from the late 18th century onward. But other Western developments—for example, such as new attitudes toward children—might come with somewhat greater difficulty. The European package—the Western model, if you will—was increasingly complicated, and this would affect responses to Western activities in the wider world, as well.

Lecture Twenty-Two
The Rise of Russia

Scope:

Russia poses a bit of a problem for world historians. Is it a civilization all its own or part of a slightly larger East European civilization? Should it be handled, as is commonly the case in European history texts, as part of Europe, though not a leading part? And how important is Russia? Developments in the early modern period, crucial in Russian history per se, suggest the need to treat Russia separately but with a clear asterisk; they also suggest the importance of Russian expansion on the world history stage. Early modern Russia warrants attention as an unusually durable example of the phenomenon of gunpowder empires; as a society increasingly influential in Middle Eastern and Asian, as well as European, history; and as a first instance of selective Westernization, an example of a pattern that would resound more widely in world history later on, providing, among other things, a comparative benchmark.

Outline

I. The early modern centuries saw a significant rise of Russia in world affairs, along with important changes in Russian political and cultural patterns.

    A. Categorizing Russia is a bit of a problem for world historians.

        1. In these lectures, we have defined Russia and, possibly, a larger Eastern European zone as a distinct civilization, although new relationships Russia developed with the West in the early modern period blur this distinction somewhat.

        2. An East European zone existed beyond Russia's borders—sharing with Russia, in some cases, commitment to Orthodox Christianity and to some common agricultural systems.

II. The primary Russian theme in this period was territorial expansion.

    A. Between 1450 and 1750, Russian territory expanded steadily in several directions, not yet reaching its current dimensions but, without question, creating a substantial gunpowder empire.

    B. One factor that pushed Russia to expansion was the desire to drive the Mongols further away.

    C. Russia was also driven by the idea of itself as the heir to the Byzantine Empire.

    D. Along with this notion was some sense of a religious mission. Russia frequently insisted that it had a role to play in the Middle East in defense of Christianity, especially Orthodox Christianity.

    E. As the early modern period progressed, the Russian state and individual groups, such as the Cossacks, also developed a direct stake in expansion. Expansion was one of the ways in which the tsars could justify their rule; other groups sought new opportunities to obtain land.

    F. Expansion took several directions. The most important expansion was southward into Central Asia and to the borders of the Ottoman Empire. Here, Russia began to influence world affairs in fundamental ways.

        1. By the 17th and 18th centuries, Russian-Ottoman conflict increasingly moved to the advantage of the Russians. Russia was involved in pushing the Ottoman Empire back, gaining new territories to the south and the southeast in the process.

        2. Russian expansion also eliminated Central Asia and its nomadic groups as an independent factor in Eurasian affairs. Russian expansion, along with Chinese and Ottoman expansion, increasingly placed most of Central Asia under the control of an organized state.

        3. Russian expansion began to produce a Muslim minority in Russia. Although Russia cast itself as a European state, the tsar presented himself as a ruler who operated in a Muslim tradition.

G. The second direction of Russian expansion was westward, when Russia began to move into Ukraine and other territories that brought it directly into East-Central European affairs.

    1. By the end of the 17th century, Russia played a role in military and diplomatic interactions with such countries as Sweden, Prussia, and Austria-Hungary. After about 1750, Russia would assume a more general role in European diplomacy.

    2. This push westward brought new minorities into Russian rule, including Jews and German ethnic minorities.

H. The third direction of Russian expansion was eastward, across the Ural Mountains into Siberia and, ultimately, even beyond. By the 18th century, this move brought Russia into direct contact with China.

    1. The mid-18th-century Amur River Treaty established a border between China and Russia that indicated the extent to which Russia was now a minor player in East Asian affairs.

    2. During the 18th century, Russia pressed beyond East Asia into Alaska, and Russian explorers moved south from Alaska into present-day northern California.

    3. Russian trading expeditions even reached the northernmost island of Hawaii.

I. By 1750, Russia had one of the largest landmasses under single rule that had ever existed. This expansion established Russia as a multinational society at the same time that Western Europe was emphasizing the nation state. This multinational quality would be both a strength of and a challenge to Russia from this point onward.

J. This expansion also established Russia as a frontier society, particularly in the east but also in parts of Central Asia.

III. Two devices were used in the early modern period to hold the Russian territory together.

    A. The first device was the strong assertion of the power of the central state and its ruler, the tsar, but state authority was often hollow.

B. The second device was, essentially, an agreement between the state and the landlord class.

    1. Both big landlords and gentry-level landlords were given increasing political and economic powers to run local courts, administer justice, punish criminals, levy taxes, and require labor service from serfs.

    2. This decentralization into estate-based management gave Russia the opportunity to establish at least some political stability even in its huge new territories.

C. Once in a while, this agreement between the tsar and his nobles broke down and trouble ensued. For the most part, however, the agreement held steady because both parties had a stake in preserving this system.

IV. In the later-17th century, Russia embarked on another important pattern of change: Westernization.

    A. Peter the Great decided that to maintain Russia's military mission and to further Russia's goals of becoming a European power, significant changes had to occur involving Russia's imitation of patterns then visible in the West.

    B. Westernization reforms under Peter took several directions. One set of changes was what we might call cosmetic.

        1. Peter insisted that his nobles trim off their Mongol-like beards and adopt Western dress, rather than Asian.

        2. Western cultural institutions were imported into Russia, notably, the ballet.

        3. These various changes added up to a major effort to alter Russia's cultural orientation in significant directions.

    C. The second set of changes involved efforts to improve Russian education, particularly for the upper classes, and scientific work.

        1. Under Peter, new scientific academies and universities were established, including the State University of St. Petersburg.

        2. All nobles were to receive training in mathematics; they would not be allowed to marry if they did not obtain an educational certificate.

D. The third set of changes was political and fairly straightforward. Peter developed somewhat more specialized bureaucratic services and created a state counsel to oversee bureaucratic activities.

E. Peter instituted significant, though not uniform, military and economic changes.

    1. He established a Russian navy, importing Western artisans and advisors to do so. He tried to improve the armament of the Russian army, and reorganized the army into somewhat clearer categories of command along partially Western lines.

    2. He also organized the Russian metallurgical industry, taking advantage of Russia's holdings in iron ore to build an economic basis for independent weapons productions and to equip Russia's armies without having to rely on Western imports.

V. What were the goals of Peter's program of Westernization?

A. The first goal was to enhance the power of the tsar and the state in what was still a fairly ineffective state apparatus.

B. The second goal was to enhance the power of the Russian military so that it could play a role in European affairs and would have an edge in its military conflicts elsewhere, specifically, with the Ottoman Empire.

C. The third goal was to address what one might call an embarrassment factor with Russia vis-à-vis the West.

    1. Peter assumed that interchange between Russia and the West would become more frequent and that, without some changes, Russia would be viewed by Westerners as barbaric and backward.

    2. One way to deal with this problem was to make at least upper-class Russia look increasingly Western.

VI. Equally important, however, was what Peter the Great did not Westernize.

A. He did not import Western ideas about constitutional monarchy, the parliamentary tradition, or the division of powers.

B. Peter was not interested in any significant reforms that affected ordinary Russians.

   1. He did not ameliorate the conditions of the serfs, nor did he institute a wage labor economy in Russia.

   2. He did not try to bring cultural or educational change to ordinary Russians.

C. Perhaps most revealing of all, Peter clearly did not want to make Russia a commercial economy in the Western model. If we go back to the terms of the world economy, Peter's goal was to maintain Russia as an external economy, capable of producing what it needed for its own economic operation and for its expanding military activity but not seeking commercial dominance over areas outside of Russia.

VII. The Westernization program was quite real, but ironically enhanced some of Russia's differences with the West.

   A. Russia joined Western cultural life, and Peter the Great was obviously eager to further Russia's role as a European diplomatic and military player, but he was not interested in creating a Western society.

   B. In confirming or widening the gap between ordinary Russians and the upper classes, Peter created circumstances that were quite different from those of the West and would have different outcomes later.

   C. Peter's changes had at least two unintended consequences that, from this point onward, would inform Russian affairs and continue to differentiate Russia from the West while also connecting it to the West without any question.

   1. After Peter's death, Orthodox clergy and some landlords voiced concerns about the implications of Westernization; the result was an ongoing ambivalence about what Russia's relationship with the West should be.

   2. Although Peter intended for Russia to remain an external economy, his actions encouraged involvement in the European-dominated economy on terms that were not favorable to Russia. The desire for Western goods pushed Russia into the position of a peripheral economy, emphasizing timber, minerals, and grains in its exports and depending on serf labor.

D. Westernization probably did help maintain the military strength of the Russian imperial experiment, but it also set in motion other currents that would have further effects on Russia's relationship with the wider world—sometimes fostering new links, particularly with the West, but sometimes creating new tensions as well.

Further Reading:

Lindsey Hughes, *Peter the Great and the West: New Perspectives.*

Michael Khodarkovsky, *Russia's Steppe Frontier: The Making of a Colonial Empire, 1500–1800.*

Richard Stites, *Serfdom, Society and the Arts in Imperial Russia: The Pleasure and the Power.*

Questions to Consider:

1. What kind of relationship to the world economy did Peter the Great seek: a European-style core position, a peripheral position, or something else? What position resulted from Russia's version of Westernization over the longer term?

2. Why and how did serfdom become a dominant issue in Russian history?

Lecture Twenty-Two—Transcript
The Rise of Russia

The early modern centuries saw what is incontestably a significant rise of Russia in world affairs. It was also a period in which Russian political and cultural patterns changed significantly, as well. We need to remember—and this has come up earlier in our discussions—that Russia is a bit of a problem for world historians. I've tried to resolve the problem by an emphasis on Russia and, possibly, a larger Eastern European zone as a distinct civilization. Part of the problem, frankly, stems not from world history at all, but from an older tradition in European history that saw Russia treated in European history textbooks but often relegated to a small chapter late in the section, which frankly, hardly does justice to the significance of Russia in this period and beyond. But there are some issues here. The issues are compounded, indeed, in this period by new relationships that Russia developed with the West itself. Early in the early modern period, for example, Russian leaders, the new tsars, began to send emissaries to the West and to utilize Western artists and architects. For example, the Kremlin was designed by Italian architects, though using Russian themes to some extent. Russia's relationship with the West is one of the issues we will have to deal with in this discussion, but it was not a relationship that involved absolute identity. It remains preferable to look at Russia as a separate case.

We also, without belaboring the point, need to remember that a larger East European zone existed even beyond Russia's borders. It shared with Russia, in some cases, commitment to the Orthodox version of Christianity and to agricultural systems that had some rough points in common. The issue of an East European zone, of which Russia was now the clear leader, is something that we need to keep in mind as we turn to developments in the early modern period and beyond.

The most obvious theme—and one that's important for both Russia itself and for much of the Eurasian world—of Russia in the early modern period was territorial expansion. It didn't happen all the time; there were setbacks. But between 1450 and 1750, Russian territory expanded steadily in several directions, not yet reaching its present dimensions but without question creating an empire of substantial size. Russia was, indeed, one of the great gunpowder empires of the early modern period. In some ways, over time, it was the most successful and durable one because elements of the empire still exist, and we need to look at that vantage point for Russia, as well.

It's not totally easy to identify what factors pushed Russia to expansion. Without question, one early one—and we've touched on it before—involved the issue of trying to drive the Mongols further away, pressing further into Central Asia in order to keep the Mongol threat at bay. That could at least be an initial stimulus to expansion. Russia was also moved, at least rhetorically, by the notion that Russia had become the heir to the Byzantine Empire. The notion of Russia as the third Rome—first, the Roman Empire itself; then, Byzantium; and then, Russia, again, whose tsar had carefully married one of the last heiresses of the Byzantine throne—the notion of Russia inheriting an imperial mantle may not have justified all the expansion, but [it] certainly provided an interesting rhetorical cover. There was also, periodically—and this could relate to the Byzantine idea—some sense of religious mission. Russia, for example, would frequently insist that it had some role to play in the Middle East in defense of Christianity and, particularly, in defense of Orthodox Christianity. A number of motives were in play.

It was also true that as the early modern period progressed, the Russian state itself developed a direct stake in expansion. Expansion was one of the ways the tsars could justify their rule to themselves and others. Many individual Russians, both landowners seeking new territories—particularly to the east—and more ordinary Russians, seeking new land opportunities themselves—groups such as the Cossacks, who were used so actively in expansion—these individual groups developed a stake in expansion, as well.

Expansion took several directions. Most important during much of this period was the expansion southward into Central Asia and to the borders of the Ottoman Empire. Here, Russia began to influence world affairs in two fundamental ways, with a third issue also interesting. There was the direct contact with the Ottoman Empire. By the 17th and certainly the 18th centuries, recurrent Russian-Ottoman conflict increasingly moved to the advantage of the Russians. Russia was involved in pressing the Ottoman Empire and gradually pushing it back, gaining new territories to the south and, to some extent, the southeast in the process.

The second huge change that Russian expansion in this direction involved was the elimination, at least for a long period, of Central Asia as an independent factor in Eurasian affairs. You will easily remember, at so many points in our discussions to date, that the nomadic groups of Central Asia played such a tremendous role recurrently in migrations, invasion, and trade connections among major societies. Russian expansion, along with some Chinese and Ottoman expansion, now increasingly placed most of Central Asia under the control, at least nominally, of an organized state. The independent action of Central Asian nomads began to diminish. Central Asia, indeed, became something of an internal colony for the Russians, providing opportunities to gain raw materials, gain access to products that would then feed a larger development of the Russian economy. It was a very important development in larger world historical terms.

The same expansion, finally [and] quite obviously, began to produce a significant Muslim minority in Russia itself. The tsar during the early modern period was very careful to present himself to his Muslim subjects as a Muslim ruler—or, at least, as a ruler that operated in a Muslim tradition. He didn't claim to be Muslim directly. This partly allowed the tsar to continue to call on some of the Mongol precedents. Although Russia was increasingly casting itself as a European state, the Mongol precedent was not entirely forgotten, but the interaction between the Russian state, the majority Russian population, and this growing Muslim minority was an interesting development at the time. It obviously continues to play a major role in Russian affairs to the present day.

The second direction of Russian expansion was, obviously, westward. It started a little later but was nevertheless marked. Russia began to move into Ukraine, into other territories that brought it directly into East-Central European affairs. By the end of the 17th century, Russia was playing a role in military and diplomatic interactions with countries such as Sweden, Prussia, and Austria-Hungary, some of the major players in this part of Europe. Soon, although more after 1750 than before, Russia would assert a role in European diplomacy more generally. This push westward also brought new minorities into Russian rule. A significant Jewish population was acquired, particularly as Russia moved into Polish territory. German ethic minorities played an important role in Russian activities.

The third direction of Russian expansion was eastward, across the Ural Mountains into Siberia and, ultimately, even beyond. This brought Russia, by the 18th century, into direct contact with China. A mid-18th-century treaty, the Amur River Treaty, established a border between China and Russia that turned out not to be eternal but did indicate the extent to which Russia was now a minor player in East Asian, as well as central West Asian and European affairs. During the 18th century, Russia pressed beyond East Asia proper into Alaska, and Russian explorers moved south from Alaska down into present-day northern California. Russian trading expeditions even reached the northernmost island of Hawaii, where remnants of two Russian forts still exist. This was, clearly, a truly expansionist society, creating, by 1750, one of the largest landmasses under single rule that had ever existed before. This expansion created—and we've touched on the implicit point here already—Russia as a multinational society, interestingly, at the very time that Western Europe was increasingly emphasizing the nation-state. This multinational quality would be both a strength and a challenge to Russia from this point onward.

This expansion also created Russia as a frontier society, an element that I think we too often forget. Russia had significant frontier conditions, particularly in the east, but also in parts of Central Asia. Pioneering activity, cowboy-like developments, are an important part of Russian history, certainly by the 17th and 18th centuries. This was one reason that, in the 19th century, the great French observer Alexis de Tocqueville would so liken developments in Russia to those in the United States. They were two giant societies, two societies exploring their frontiers, a relationship that remains interesting to contemplate even, again, to the present day.

Russian expansion had one other consequence quite clearly, familiar enough from other world history expansions previously. That was the question of how to hold this thing together. Two devices were particularly used in the early modern period. First of all was a strong assertion of the power of the central state and its ruler, the tsar— Russian for "Caesar," again, the connection with the idea of the third Rome. State authority was widely asserted, but frankly, it was often fairly hollow, because the key device for holding this vast territory together, or at least much of it, depended on, essentially, an agreement between the Russian state and the landlord class. There were both big landlords and gentry-level landlords who were given increasing powers over Russian peasants, the serfs, political as well as economic power—power to run local courts, power to administer justice, power to punish criminals, as well as power to levy taxation and labor service. This decentralization into an estate-based management provided Russia the opportunity to establish at least nominal political stability even in its huge new territories. It was not explicitly inconsistent with the idea of a powerful tsar as well, so long as the tsar and his major nobles managed to agree. Once in a while, that agreement broke down and times of trouble ensued, but for the most part, it held steady because both parties, both the tsar and the great nobles, had a stake in preserving this system. Russian serfdom, then, which was a new development in this period— Russian peasants in the postclassical period had been relatively free—Russian serfdom in this period has to be seen then as, first of all, a major development in its own right but, second, as a response to political, as well as economic conditions.

In the later 17th century, Russia embarked on another pattern of change that was truly important at the time and is fascinating in its analytical implications. It calls upon us to assess, once again, the relationship between Russia and other parts of Europe, and it calls upon us, as well, to assess the first instance of a phenomenon that would show up at other places later in world history, the phenomenon of Westernization. The basic facts are pretty simple: A new tsar in the late 17th century, Peter the Great, decided that in order to maintain Russia's military mission, in order to further Russia's goals of being seen as a European power and not primarily an Asian power, significant changes had to occur that would involve Russia's imitation of patterns then visible in the West. Peter the Great, clearly one of the great characters—not necessarily one of the nice characters but one of the great characters of world history, almost seven feet tall—had himself traveled to the West, particularly to the Netherlands. He had worked as a shipbuilding artisan to learn techniques in this area. He obviously was deeply imbued with the sense that the West had a lot to offer Russia that he, as tsar, needed to impose.

Westernization reforms under Peter took several directions. First—and these are in no particular order of priority—were what one might call cosmetic changes. Peter the Great insisted that his nobles trim off their Mongol-like beards and adopt Western rather than Asian dress. Famous cartoons in the period actually have Peter himself trimming the beards of somewhat reluctant nobleman. Upper-class women were also urged to dress in Western fashion, and every indication is that they were happier about this change than some of the men were. Western cultural institutions were imported into Russia. Notably, for example, the ballet, fundamentally a French dance form, was imported into Russia and became so deeply anchored there that it became known almost as a Russian institution. Western art was encouraged. Other aspects of Western cultural presence were encouraged from Peter the Great onward. Cultural change in the cosmetic or aesthetic directions was truly important. Another interesting example that I find intriguing was the importation of the German custom of using fir trees at Christmastime. Russia adopted the Christmas tree a century or more before it would be adopted in other parts of Western Europe and the United States. They are little things but adding up to a significant effort to switch Russia's cultural orientation in significant directions.

The second set of changes—also cultural, broadly construed, but with much clearer purpose—involved efforts to improve Russian education, particularly for the upper classes, and Russian scientific work. Under Peter, new universities were established. The State University of St. Petersburg, still one of the major institutions in Russia, was established at the end of Peter the Great's reign. Scientific academies were set up. Sometimes, they debated scientific and technological changes that nobody was really interested in implementing in Russia. Nevertheless, an apparatus for joining Russia to a broader European scientific community was unquestionably established. Peter the Great decreed that all nobles should receive training in mathematics, at pain, at least on paper, of not being allowed to marry if they didn't obtain an educational certificate. There were lots of changes here designed, obviously, to improve Russia's scientific and technical capacity and improve the training of the people who would serve as Peter the Great's bureaucrats. Those were the second set of changes.

The third set of changes was political, pretty straightforward. Peter the Great was obviously interested in some of the new specialization and training institutions associated with absolute monarchy in Western and Central Europe. He developed somewhat more specialized bureaucratic services. He created a state counsel to oversee bureaucratic activities. I don't mean they are trivial, but these were pretty obvious things for an aspiring authoritarian ruler to import to make his rule more clear-cut.

Finally, Peter the Great instituted significant, though not uniform, military and economic changes. He established a Russian navy, importing Western artisans and advisors to do so. He tried to improve the armament of the Russian army, as well as reorganizing it into somewhat clearer-cut categories of command, again, along partially Western lines. He also was eager to organize the Russian metallurgical industry, taking advantage of Russia's terrific holdings in iron ore, so that Russia would have the economic basis for independent weapons production [and] would be able to maintain a significant level of military armament at a reasonably high technical level without having to rely, on an ongoing basis, on Western imports.

These changes added up to a desire to enhance the power of the tsar by insisting not only on new bureaucratic reforms to make the state more efficient but even by insisting on the tsar's right to cut off the beard of a nobleman. What better way, symbolically, to make it very clear that the nobles were subordinate to the rule of the tsar than to argue that the tsar could determine what they were supposed to look like?

Goal number one was to enhance the power of the tsar and the state in what was still a fairly ineffective state apparatus. Goal number two, quite clear, was to enhance the power of the Russian military, so that it could, indeed, play a role in European affairs and so it would have an increasing edge in its military conflicts elsewhere— particularly with the Ottoman Empire. Probably the most concrete result of Russia's Westernization at this point was, indeed, to make this gunpowder empire increasingly effective, one of the reasons that it would prove so durable.

Goal number three is really intriguing because it's something that happened at this point in Russia and would happen in other places later on. Goal number three was to deal with what one might call an embarrassment factor with Russia vis-à-vis the West. Peter the Great obviously assumed that interchange between Russia and the West would become increasingly frequent. He needed Western advisors; he was encouraging Western intellectual imports. But in the process, it became very clear that without some additional changes, Russia was going to be looked at by the Westerners as barbaric and backward. How to deal with this? Make at least upper-class Russia look increasingly Western. One of the interesting specific changes that Peter the Great introduced, for example, was the elimination of a Russian tradition whereby when a young woman got married, her father would hand a whip to the groom—a symbol of the transfer of male authority over women. This blow for greater female independence certainly pleased upper-class women in Russia, but it also was another way in which Peter was trying to make at least the appearances of upper-class society more palatable in Western eyes.

Equally important, however, was what Peter the Great did not Westernize. He obviously did not import increasingly current Western ideas about constitutional monarchy, the importance of parliament, and the importance of division in powers. This was of no interest. It wasn't yet dominant in the West itself, in fairness, but he could have picked it up in Holland. Undoubtedly, he was aware of it. He had no interest in it. It contradicted the purposes that he had in mind. He was not interested either in any significant reforms that affected ordinary Russians. He did not ameliorate the conditions of the serfs. He did not try to make Russia an increasingly wage labor economy. He did not try to bring cultural change to ordinary Russians. He did not change the educational apparatus, which was frankly minimal, of ordinary Russians. He did not challenge the hold of Orthodox Christianity on ordinary Russians because he had no interest in doing so. This would have undermined his authority and would have roused resistances that he had no interest in encountering. Perhaps most revealing of all, he clearly did not want to make Russia a commercial kind of economy along the Western model. He wanted economic change, he wanted a production basis for successful and independent military activity, but he did not particularly encourage the merchant class. He was content to rely heavily on Western enclaves of merchants in Moscow and in his new city of St. Petersburg to organize the bulk of Russia's trade with the West. Landlords, among other things, would have resisted—did resist—any move to enhance merchant power because they saw this as a threat to their own social and political superiority. In fact, if we can go back to the terms of the world economy, Peter's goal—although he didn't know the term—was actually to maintain Russia as an external economy, capable of producing what it needed for its own economic operation and for its expanding military activity without depending on other areas but not seeking commercial dominance over other areas outside of Russia itself, not seeking a core status in any real way at all.

These developments, in other words, created significant change in Russia. The Westernization was quite real but also, in an ironic way, enhanced Russia's differences with the West at the same time. This was a Russia that did join Western cultural life, not yet as a major producer, but within a century, it would be producing literature, music, and some art that entered the general European orbit. Peter the Great was obviously eager to enhance Russia's role as a European diplomatic and military player. This, too, would expand over time. But, again, he was not interested—he was deliberately uninterested—in creating a Western society. That would not have suited his purposes, which were quite selective. In confirming, indeed, enhancing, the gap, for example, between ordinary Russians and the Russian upper classes, Peter the Great created circumstances that were quite different from those of the West and would have different outcomes later on. Most obviously, by encouraging upper-class Russians to be increasingly Western in their ways—by the middle of the 18th century, some Russian noblemen did not speak Russian at all; they only spoke French—by increasing their Westernization while confirming the inferiority and servitude of ordinary Russians, Peter created a social gap that was quite different from that which existed in much of Western Europe. There were social tensions there, as well, but they didn't involve this depth of cultural divide. A different product was being created.

Finally, Peter the Great's changes had at least two unintended consequences that, from this point onward, would also help inform Russian affairs and, on the whole, continue to differentiate Russia from the West per se, while connecting it to the West without any question. First, although Peter's reforms did not produce a huge outcry during his own reign—his power was too great to permit this—after his death and the arrival of weaker successors, a number of voices were raised against what Peter had done. They were coming particularly from the Orthodox clergy, who were quite worried about the implications of Westernization, but coming from some landlords and others, as well. The result, in Russia as a whole and sometimes in the individual Russian leaders themselves, was a real ongoing ambivalence as to what Russia's relationship with the West should be. Should Russia become more Western than Peter intended? Some of the noblemen who now visited the West would argue yes. The West was the model and Russia's mistake was simply not going far enough. Or should Russia pull back because core Russian values were actually superior to those of the West and Peter the Great's flirtation was, in fact, a great danger? The ambiguity with regard to the Western relationship was something that would crop up recurrently in Russian history from this point onward. Early in the 19th century, during the Soviet era—and, I think, arguably, at the turn of the 21st century, as well—it becomes a durable or, at least, recurrent feature of the Russian cultural character.

The second unintended consequence was also fascinating. While Peter—again, if I could be permitted to use the world economic terms—intended Russia to remain external, what he did actually encouraged some further involvement with Russia in the European-dominated economy on terms that were not terribly favorable to Russia itself. Most obviously, despite Peter the Great's interest in seeing the Russian economy remain independent of the West, more and more upper-class Russians thirsted for Western goods. They wanted increasing numbers of Western paintings of the sort that would ultimately accumulate in one of the great collections of Western art anywhere in the world in St. Petersburg. They wanted growing amounts of Western furniture. They wanted Western lecturers. They wanted Western access in various sorts. It became a standard feature in the life of a young nobleman to have a grand tour of the West that could last many months, even years. These appetites for Western-type goods cost money. Along with the continued need to import certain kinds of equipment from the West, they created a new balance-of-payments situation in which Russia was pressed increasingly to augment its export patterns to the West by emphasizing timber products, minerals, and particularly, grains. Russia became, by the later 18th century and on into the 19th century, one of the great grain suppliers for Western markets, depending on serfial labor, depending on increasingly harsh serfial labor, in fact, as punishments and restrictions over the peasantry steadily expanded. This smacked increasingly if not of a peripheral economy, at least of an economy that was somewhat peripheral. It was not as different, say, from Latin America as Peter the Great and other Russian leaders might have aspired to.

This, then, was an important set of moves. It probably did help maintain the strength—particularly the military strength—of the Russian imperial experiment. Again, of all the great gunpowder empires created in the early modern period, Russia has had the most lasting success in maintaining at least much of its expanded territories intact. But these developments also set other new currents in motion in Russia that would have further effects on Russia's relationship with the wider world—sometimes creating new links, particularly with the West, but sometimes creating new tensions as Russians might spring back against too much Western linkage. It's a process that, again, would be set in motion and would crop up from time to time on into the present day.

Lecture Twenty-Three
Asian Empires and a Shogunate

Scope:

Key changes marked the experience of the leading Asian societies during the early modern centuries, changes that had little to do with developments in the West or Russia. The Asian continent, although involved in the world economy, was long buffered from its worst pressures. The formation of new empires—the Ottoman, the Safavid, and the Mughal—brought significant cultural and political changes. In China, a more familiar dynastic cycle saw the Ming rise and decline, to be replaced by the nation's final dynasty, the Qing. By the 18th century, however, several of the Asian gunpowder empires were faltering. The Mughal Empire was in serious trouble, though technically it survived into the 19th century. The Ottoman Empire passed its expansionist prime in the 17th century, though it retained great power. The situation in China was more complex, but there were signs of new difficulties by the 18th century. Each imperial pattern had its own dynamic and characteristics, but it is legitimate to ask if there were some shared issues. Finally, Japan, though not an empire, experienced significant change as well, important at the time and for the future.

Outline

I. Lumping together the Asian societies in the early modern period is presumptuous.

   A. The territory of Asian civilization is huge, encompassing a number of different societies, but a few generalizations are possible to help round out our understanding of the early modern centuries.

   B. Contrary to longstanding presumptions, most Asian societies in this period were actively engaged in wider connections in the world, although on different terms from those that operated in the West.

II. We can identify two major developments in Asian societies during the early modern period.

    A. The first development was increasing prosperity, at least for some groups, as a result of Asia's participation in production for world markets in exchange for American silver. This participation confirms, among other things, an interest in export-based manufacture in parts of China and an interest in transmission to world markets in India.

    B. The second development was the emergence of a series of gunpowder empires in much of the Asian landmass.

        1. The Ottoman Empire began to take shape in the middle of the 15th century and extended its hold over much of southeastern Europe. It developed significant holdings in much of the Middle East, extended its direct control to Egypt, and had some nominal control over other parts of North Africa, though not Morocco.

        2. The Mughal Empire emerged in India in the early-16th century as a result of invasions from a force that operated through Afghanistan.

        3. The Safavid Empire in Persia was a smaller gunpowder empire that helped revive a sense of Persian identity and presence and maintained significance for a couple of centuries.

    C. China, where the imperial tradition was well established, operated according to a somewhat different rhythm. Much of the early modern period saw the operation of the Ming dynasty, followed by the Qing dynasty, which had some elements of gunpowder empire attached to it, as well.

        1. The Qing had been organized by Manchurians coming in from northern China and remained partially outside Chinese culture.

        2. This element was not dissimilar to other gunpowder empires, in which an intrusion from outside helped to shape the imperial experience more generally.

III. These empires had significant accomplishments, although they were not quite as dynamic as those occurring in Western Europe.

    A. Asian power began to decline a bit in this period if measured against European power. The longstanding trend in which technological leadership and innovation centered in Asia, particularly East Asia, and tended to move westward began to shift toward greater Western parity and even slight leadership.

B. The Ottoman Empire brought a number of developments to the Middle East and southeastern Europe, solidifying and highlighting a new Turkish presence in the northern Middle East. But Ottoman administration was never purely Turkish: it incorporated a number of other peoples, including non-Muslims.

    1. The Ottoman Empire helped encourage the spread of Islamic belief to parts of southeastern Europe, although Christian groups were, for the most part, tolerated.

    2. The Ottoman regime also confirmed a dependent and inferior political status for Arabs.

    3. The Ottoman Empire introduced cultural changes into the Middle East: a form of mosque developed that blended Byzantine architectural forms with Muslim needs; Ottoman contributions to literature and art, often in Arabic, were also significant.

C. Mughal contributions to India were numerous. At its high point, the Mughal Empire encompassed a system of considerable tolerance and a mixture of Hindus and Muslims.

    1. The Mughals introduced additional cultural richness into the Indian tradition, including Persian and Western artistic influences as well as important individual symbols such as the Taj Mahal.

    2. The Mughals promoted the possibility of creating larger territorial units in the Indian subcontinent, which would feed directly into Indian unity after the passing of British rule.

    3. The Mughals developed administrative and taxation structures that had lasting impact in India.

    4. The Mughals were interested in reforming certain traditional Indian practices, such as the practice of *sati*, though results here were meager.

D. Developments in Safavid Persia included a revival of a sense of Persian identity. It was under the Safavid Empire, for example, that Farsi was established as the dominant language of the region.

E. Developments in Qing China included economic prosperity and the re-elaboration of the bureaucratic imperial state. Significant population expansion occurred under the very late Ming dynasty and the Qing.

F. During much of the early modern period, Asian empires—largely independent of Western influence in any cultural or political sense—made important achievements that would outlast the empires themselves.

IV. Some of the gunpowder empires began to show signs of wear as early as the late-17th or early-18th centuries.

    A. The Safavid Empire began to weaken in the early-18th century, and the Mughal Empire began to weaken even somewhat earlier. If their goal was to preserve Indian vitality and Mughal rule, then later-17th-century Mughal emperors made two mistakes.

        1. Several later emperors began to reverse the policy of religious tolerance, clearly favoring Muslims in administration and creating an atmosphere of religious mistrust.

        2. The second mistake was overexpansion. The attempt to press Mughal boundaries southward led to significant military expenditure at the expense of the taxation base and the basic economic vitality of India as a whole.

    B. By the 18th century, Mughal hold over India began to fade in favor of local princes, and Indian economic prosperity declined. It was in this context that European powers, ultimately led by the English, began to interfere in Indian affairs.

        1. The British East India Company took advantage of Mughal weakness to establish a beachhead on the continent.

        2. The later-18th century saw the increasing conversion of much of India to, essentially, a British colony.

C. The Ottoman Empire presents a different picture. This regime reached a high point in the late-16th and 17th centuries. A last effort at territorial expansion occurred in the 1680s, as Ottoman troops twice attacked Vienna, hoping to press farther into Central Europe. These attacks failed and, from that point onward, the Ottomans suffered territorial setbacks.

    1. These setbacks pressed the empires in other ways: It became harder to reward loyal bureaucrats and generals. Many parts of the empire were parceled out among chief administrators who might meld the provinces for personal advantage. Corruption and economic dislocation increased.

    2. Nonetheless, the Ottoman Empire remained healthy well into the 19th century.

    3. By the 18th century, sensing Ottoman weakness and undoubtedly exploiting an older prejudice against Islam, European opinion began to hold that Ottoman rule was both sick and weak. This perception would create a reality of its own during the 19th century and affect Europe's relations with the Middle East.

D. Developments in China were much more complex. In most fundamental respects, the Chinese state and economy remained vigorous up until the 1830s, but there were some modest signs of trouble.

    1. Probably by the 18th century, China began to be burdened by overpopulation that would affect larger economic dynamism and growth.

    2. At the same time, China ceased being a source of major technological innovation, and cultural creativity lagged.

    3. The empire may also have been affected by excessive bureaucratization that made decision-making difficult and communication with the provinces cumbersome.

V. These empires, particularly China and the Ottoman Empire, did not look to selective developments in the West as a model for certain reforms, as Russia had done.

A. China had been open to modest Western activity in much of the early modern period, but this openness turned sour in the early-18th century. Participation in trade remained vigorous, but there was, if anything, a withdrawal from an interest in contacts of other sorts.

B. The Ottoman Empire rather systematically avoided the possibility of influential imports from the West.

    1. The printing press was banned from the empire until the middle of the 18th century, when it was first allowed only for Christians, not Muslims. This was an obvious attempt by the government to control access to information and ideology.

    2. The only Western influence directly incorporated by Ottoman rulers, interestingly enough, was Western doctors, who were called upon to service the Ottoman court.

C. For most of the early modern period, significant achievements were registered in Asia, but these gains were somewhat overshadowed by the greater vigor of developments in the West.

VI. Japan contrasts to some extent with the developments in the gunpowder empires we have seen thus far.

    A. The early modern period was a crucial one in Japanese history. After some flirtation with Western contacts, Japanese leaders decided at the end of the 16th century to close off contacts and emphasize internal economic, political, and cultural development.

    B. This period became known as the Tokugawa shogunate, which would last until 1868.

        1. Under the shogunate, the ritual apparatus of feudalism was carefully preserved, along with the social privileges of feudal lords.

        2. Alongside feudalism was the apparatus of a small but definite central state.

        3. The shogunate was the framework for the successful expansion of commercial activity in Japan.

    C. The Japanese turned increasingly to Confucianism during the early modern period.

        1. As Confucianism spread, this-worldly concerns began to predominate in Japanese culture, along with new artistic forms that would mark further steps in Japanese cultural identity.

  2. Japan also saw an increasing commitment to education, not just for the upper class but for broader bands of society. Over time, Japanese Confucianism encouraged an educational commitment that would position Japan as the second society, after the West, in literacy rates by the early-19th century.

D. The Japanese population did not grow massively during the 18th century. The fairly extensive use of abortion, among other things, seems to have limited Japanese population growth.

E. Also important for the future of Japan was the tendency in the 18th century to become slightly more open to outside influences. This interest indicated that the Japanese were aware of developments in the outside world and saw a need to find out what these developments might portend.

VII. The patterns we have discussed in this lecture do not overturn conventional views of Asian history in the early modern period entirely.

A. Relative decline is undeniable, but it must not overwhelm our understanding that important positive developments took place during much of this period.

B. At the same time, we should note the decline of specific regimes, most notably in Mughal India. But the sense that Asia began to be backward or isolated in this period is simply wrong.

C. World historians, particularly experts on Asia and the world economy, have insisted that we need to redress this impression of Asian economic inferiority and backwardness.

  1. One reason for this insistence is, presumably, that it is better to be accurate than not.

  2. Another reason is that our misguided impressions pander to older Western prejudices about Asian characteristics.

  3. Asia remained a vital contributor to world history up until at least the 18th century and even into the 19th and would again become a vital contributor by the 20th century.

Further Reading:

Rifa'at Abou-El-Haj, *Formation of the Modern State: The Ottoman Empire, Sixteenth to Eighteenth Centuries.*

Catherine Asher and Cynthia Talbot, *India Before Europe.*

D. E. Mungello, *The Great Encounter of China and the West, 1500–1800.*

Questions to Consider:

1. Did the Asian societies make a serious mistake in long ignoring and, in some cases, avoiding Western patterns of change in the early modern period?

2. Why and in what ways was Mughal decline more serious than the issues emerging in other Asian societies by the 18th century?

Lecture Twenty-Three—Transcript
Asian Empires and a Shogunate

Our focus in this discussion is on Asian societies during the early modern period. Frankly, it's a presumptuous combination. This is a huge territory with all sorts of different societies that experienced all sorts of different developments during this long period, but a few generalizations are possible, and they will help round out our understanding of what was going on during these interesting centuries.

One of the first things to emphasize is the extent to which attention, even brief, to Asian developments in the early modern period needs to fight longstanding prejudices and stereotypes. Many of my students, who sometimes don't seem to know a lot about world history when they come into to my class, nevertheless do know that China was isolated and conservative, and this set of characteristics seems to dominate some impressions of China, at least before recent times.

This was a period in which most Asian societies were actively engaged in wider connections in the world on different terms from those that operated in Western Europe, to be sure. This was not, in the main, an isolationist period. This was not a period of economic retrenchment. The necessity of confronting some of these misimpressions head-on is one of the crucial reasons to deal with this wide-ranging topic in a specific session. We'll return at the end to the question of why it's so important to rectify the record, and many world historians have actively contributed to this task.

Again, trying to look at the big picture with regard to a number of different societies, there were two big developments in Asian societies during the early modern period. The first development, which we already touched on in dealing with the absolute necessity of modifying the world economy approach where Asia is concerned, was increasing prosperity, at least for some groups, as a result of Asia's participation in producing for world markets and receiving goods, including American silver, in exchange. As we noted, a number of Asian societies were significantly altered by this growing commercialization. Merchants gained new roles; money use gained new roles; governments gained access to additional resources themselves. This participation in global patterns yielding, again, at least selective prosperity, was a significant development in its own right, confirming, among other things, an interest in export-based manufacture in parts of China, an interest in transmission to world markets in parts of India, etc.

The second development, which we've also mentioned but not fully fleshed out, was the emergence of a series of gunpowder empires in much of the Asian landmass. We will also be dealing today with a somewhat separate set of developments in Japan, which don't quite fit the gunpowder empire model, but the emergence of a number of quite solid empires operating over a considerable period of time is a really interesting set of parallelisms in Asian history during this period.

The new empires were three in number—in addition, of course, to Russia, which itself established a significant Asian presence during this period. First came the Ottomans. The Ottoman Empire began to take shape in the middle of the 15th century. It's one of the factors that helped launch the early modern period. It extended its hold over much of southeastern Europe, including at the high point, even Hungary. It developed significant holdings in much of the Middle East, though not all of it. It extended its direct control to Egypt and had some nominal control over other parts of North Africa, though not Morocco. This was a major and, in fact, long-lasting empire. It outlived the Roman Empire, among other things, if you just count years.

The second empire to emerge, also extremely important, this one developing in the early 16th century, was the Mughal Empire in India. The Mughal Empire was formed as a result of invasions from a force that operated through Afghanistan. Early Mughal emperors were extremely interested in establishing a solidly based imperial structure in India. They were frequently extremely intelligent. They were interested in new ideas. They were eager to combine traditional Indian practices with new elements. They were explicitly extremely tolerant in religion. They utilized Hindus, as well as Muslims, in administration. This was a rich period in Indian history under Mughal control. Here, too, the empire expanded considerably territorially. It never controlled the entire Indian subcontinent, but it did command an increasing chunk in north and central India and even attempted, to some extent, to reach south.

The third great gunpowder empire, though a smaller one, was the Safavid Empire in Persia, which helped revive a sense of Persian identity and presence. Still Muslim, there was no overall cultural change here. This empire had a significant existence for a couple of centuries.

China, of course, operated according to a somewhat different rhythm because here the imperial tradition was well established. Much of the early modern period saw the operation of the Ming dynasty, established a bit before the early modern period, but as we've noted briefly before, the second dynasty of the early modern period—and, in fact, what turned out to be China's last dynasty—had a few elements of gunpowder empire attached to it, as well. This final dynasty, the Qing, formerly known as the Manchu, was organized by Manchurians coming in from northern China. While they adopted Chinese institutional patterns and culture in many ways, they remained partially outsiders in their own estimation and in that of the Chinese. There was in China, as well, an element that was not dissimilar to the other gunpowder empires, involving an intrusion from outside helping to shape the imperial experience more generally.

These empires had significant accomplishments. It is obviously valid to note—as, for example, Chinese observers have in looking back at this period—that the developments that occurred under the gunpowder and Chinese empires were not, overall, quite as dynamic as those occurring in Western Europe. Asian power began relatively to decline a little bit, if measured against European power. For example, by 1700, European technologies in metallurgy and in some branches of textile production were now probably superior to their Asian counterparts. They were not yet massively superior, but a balance that had been so long-standing in world history—in which technological leadership and innovation centered in Asia, particularly East Asia, and tended to move westward—this balance during the early modern period is beginning to shift toward greater Western parity and even slight leadership. It's a shift that would, obviously, be compounded in the later 18th and 19th centuries.

In talking about the achievements of the gunpowder empires, the developments in Asia in this period, both economic and political, it is important to note—at risk of encouraging stereotype, which is not my goal—that there was a certain shift in balance. Asian developments, in terms of sheer power politics and economic dynamism, were not quite keeping pace with some of the leading patterns in Europe.

Still, the gunpowder empires had significant achievements to their credit. Some textbook approaches mention the gunpowder empires and then race to their decline. We'll have to talk about their decline, at least in part, as a late early modern phenomenon, but the achievements need to be noted, in addition. The Ottoman Empire brought a number of developments to the Middle East and southeastern Europe. They obviously helped solidify and highlight a new Turkish presence in the northern Middle East, the fruit of migration, as well as political control, but it was equally important to note that Ottoman administration was never purely Turkish. It had mixed a number of other peoples, including non-Muslims, in a tradition that actually had been well established in earlier periods in the Middle East.

The Ottoman Empire helped encourage the spread of Islamic belief to a significant minority of people in parts of southeastern Europe. Christian groups were tolerated for the most part, though there were some forced conversions of a group of young military people seized as part of the Ottoman military force, the Janissaries, but the changes in the religious map in southeastern Europe were noteworthy, as well as some new antagonisms that seemed to spring up around Ottoman control.

Ottoman relationships with Arabs also deserve attention. While the Ottoman Empire used individual Arabs, as well as Christians and Jews, in administration, on the whole, the Ottoman Empire confirmed a somewhat dependent and inferior political status for Arabs, whom many Turks looked down on to some extent. That pattern has to be factored into developments in the Middle East, even to contemporary times, as well.

The Ottoman Empire introduced significant cultural changes into the Middle East. A form of mosque developed, best illustrated by some of the great mosques of Istanbul and its environs that blended, actually, Byzantine architectural forms with Muslim needs—an interesting innovation. Ottoman contributions to literature and art, often in Arabic, were also significant. Political, some religious and cultural achievements, then, left a lasting mark on the Middle East, even as the Ottoman hold would begin to decline.

Mughal contributions to India, again, were numerous. At its highpoint, a system of considerable tolerance and intermixture of Hindus and Muslims was a contribution, though unfortunately, not an entirely lasting one. Mughal cultural contributions were really major. The Mughals helped further Persian artistic influence in India, leading to new forms of portraiture. The Mughals were also interested in receiving some Western cultural influences—not deep ones, but influences that affected a style of portrait painting and even dress in the upper classes in Mughal India. Much of what we rate as Indian cuisine today dates from the Mughal period. In other worlds, the Mughals introduced significant cultural richness into the Indian tradition, as well as, of course, important individual symbols, such as the great Taj Mahal. The Mughals also, arguably, furthered a sense not of Indian unity but of the possibility of creating larger territorial units in the Indian subcontinent, which of course, the British would pick up, and then which would feed directly into considerable Indian unity after the British rule passed. This was a contribution worth noting. The Mughals also developed administrative and taxation structures that would have long impact in India, again, even after the Mughals themselves departed. Mughals were even interested, although this one didn't take, in reforming certain other traditional Indian practices—for example, the practice of *sati*, which they disapproved of but didn't ultimately have quite the clout to attack directly.

Developments in Safavid Persia included a revival of a sense of Persian identity. It was under the Safavid Empire that Farsi was established as the dominant language of the region, as it still is today in Iran. These are cultural developments that go beyond the mere fact of stating the existence of an empire.

Developments in Qing China included a significant participation in economic prosperity, the reelaboration of the bureaucratic imperial state. Significant population expansion occurred under the very late Ming and the Qing dynasty. Again, this was a pattern of developments of considerable importance. It is vital to recognize that during much of the early modern period—largely if not entirely independent of Western influence in any cultural or political sense—

Asian empires were establishing significant achievements that would leave marks that outlasted the empires themselves.

However, it is also true that some of the gunpowder empires began to show signs of wear as early as the late 17th, early 18th centuries—though the pattern is varied and we need to be careful of over-simple generalizations. The Safavid Empire began to weaken in the early 18th century. The Mughal Empire began to weaken even somewhat earlier. Later-17th-century Mughal emperors made what, in retrospect it seems, were two clear mistakes if the goal was to preserve Indian vitality and Mughal rule itself. In the first place, several later emperors began to reverse the policy of religious tolerance; began clearly to favor Muslims in administration; began, in some instances, to attack Hindu religious shrines; and began to create an atmosphere of religious mistrust that would continue to affect Indian history and be exacerbated by aspects of British rule in ways that obviously have contemporary implications, as well.

The second mistake, if this kind of historical judgment is permitted, was quite simply an effort at overexpansion. The attempt to press Mughal boundaries southward led to significant military expenditure, the amassing of vast armies, including elephant forces—sometimes successful, but at real expense to the taxation base and, indeed, the basic economic vitality of India as a whole. By the 18th century, Mughal hold over India was beginning to fade in favor of local princes, the revival of that tradition of localism so frequent in Indian politics. Indian economic prosperity was declining. Indian cultural and educational apparatus was in some disarray, as well. Of course, it was in this context, in the late 17th but particularly 18th centuries, that European powers, ultimately headed by the English, began to interfere increasingly successfully in Indian affairs. The British and, particularly, the British East India Company was able to take advantage of growing Mughal weakness to establish a growing British beachhead in the continent. The British were able to develop alliances with other Indian rulers hostile to each other or hostile to the Mughals, which furthered British rule without the commitment of vast forces. The later 18th century saw the increasing conversion of much of India to, essentially, a British colony. It was a huge change, obviously, in Indian history; it was a huge expansion of European imperial presence taking shape at the end of the early modern period.

The Ottoman Empire presents a different picture, although Europeans sometimes try to argue that it wasn't as different as it might seem. The Ottoman Empire undoubtedly reached a highpoint in the late 16th and 17th centuries. A last effort at territorial expansion occurred in the 1680s, as Ottoman troops twice attacked Vienna, hoping to press farther into Central Europe. These attacks failed, and from that point onward, the Ottomans suffered a periodic series of territorial setbacks. This was partly at the hands of Austria-Hungarians, who pressed the empire back from the Hapsburg territories, but even more at the hands of the Russians in patterns that we discussed in our previous session.

Ottoman territorial setbacks obviously pressed the empires in other ways. It became harder to reward loyal top bureaucrats and generals. Many parts of the empire became increasingly parceled out among chief administrators, who might meld the province for personal advantage. Corruption and economic dislocation increased, but the Ottoman Empire was still, in many ways, quite healthy and would remain healthy well into the 19th century. It wasn't as vibrant as it had been before. On the other hand, in no sense was it on its last legs. However, there was one further development that was interesting, as well. By the 18th century, sensing Ottoman weakness and also undoubtedly exploiting an older prejudice against Islam, European opinion began to decide that the Ottoman rule was both sick and weak. This European impression that this was an empire cruel to its subjects, cruel to women, [and] also on its last legs was a perception that would create a reality of its own during the 19th century and affect Europe's relations with the Middle East in its own right.

Developments in China were much more complex. In most fundamental respects, the Chinese state and economy remained quite vigorous up until the 1830s. For example, it was only in the 1830s and 1840s that the European balance-of-payment situation vis-à-vis China finally altered so that Europe began to be able to take precious metals from China, rather than paying them in return for Chinese goods. But there were some signs—they were modest; this is a state that's still vigorous and successful—there were some signs of trouble. Probably by the 18th century, China was beginning to be burdened by overpopulation. Fed by new food supplies, [this] overpopulation could require so many resources to sustain itself that it would affect larger economic dynamism and economic growth.

Certainly, even apart from its relative position vis-à-vis Europe, China ceased being a source of major technological innovation at this point. There's some sense, as well, that cultural creativity lagged somewhat. Chinese intellectuals were still vigorously reproducing earlier literary forms and discussing Confucian traditions. This was not a cultural collapse, but new influences, new interpretations of older themes probably declined somewhat. The empire may also have been affected by excessive bureaucratization, excessive levels of paperwork that made decision-making difficult and communication with the provinces sometimes cumbersome. Again, none of this would come home to roost still for several decades, but in retrospect, we can see some possible signs of trouble.

One thing is clear, particularly with regard to China and the Ottoman Empire, a possible source of renewal, which Russia was pursuing—albeit amid complexity, as we discussed in our previous session—was not pursued, and that was the possibility of selectively looking at developments in the West as a pattern for certain kinds of possible reforms. China, in fact, had been open to modest Western missionary activity in much of the early modern period. It had been interested—as somewhat of a curiosity but a bit more than that—in Western developments, such as clocks and other scientific discoveries. Chinese openness to even modest Western presence definitely turned sour in the early 18th century, with increasing restrictions on missionaries and persecutions of small groups of Chinese Christians. This was not a path that China chose to take. Participation in trade remained vigorous, but there was, if anything, a retreat from an interest in contacts of other sorts.

The Ottoman Empire was even more aware of developments in the West because individual Ottomans traveled frequently to Western Europe. There was no barrier of communication here at all. The Ottoman Empire also, rather systematically, avoided the possibility of influential contacts with the West. For example, the printing press, which had obviously been established in Western Europe long since, was banned from the Ottoman Empire until toward the middle of the 18th century, when it was first allowed only for Christians, not for Muslims. The reason, obviously, was not just blanket rejection of the West. The reason was a government desire to make sure, as sure as possible, that it had control over access to information and ideology. Gradually, this was loosened but pretty late in the game. The only

Western influence that was directly incorporated by Ottoman rulers, interestingly enough, was Western doctors, who were called upon to service the Ottoman court—even though, as far as one could determine, they were no more effective in actual medical practice than were the physicians in the rich traditions of the Middle East. It was a cultural fad that had no clear practical basis.

We have, then, a situation in the great states of Asia in which during most of the early modern period, significant vigor developed, significant achievements were registered, but in a pattern in which gains were somewhat overshadowed, as we now know, by the greater vigor of developments in the West. We also have a situation where—markedly to tentatively—certain signs of absolute decline begin to show, as well.

There's one final case that deserves attention that actually, to some extent, interestingly contrasts with the gunpowder empire developments we've been emphasizing thus far. The early modern period was a crucial one in Japanese history. As we've discussed previously, after some flirtation with Western contacts, Japanese leaders decided at the end of the 16th century largely to close off contacts—not entirely but largely—and emphasize a pattern of internal economic, political, and cultural development. This was the period that becomes known as the *Tokugawa shogunate*, which would last until 1868. Under the Tokugawa shogunate, feudalism persisted. The ritual apparatus of feudalism was carefully preserved, along with the social privileges of feudal lords, but alongside feudalism—and, in fact, more effective than feudalism—began to be the apparatus of a small but definite central state, serviced by its own bureaucracy, not feudal vassals, and capable of reducing—in most cases, eliminating—internal warfare and providing increasing political unity. This was, in turn, the framework for the rather successful expansion of commercial activity within Japan that we have discussed before. This was obviously a significant and, as it turned out, fairly durable political change in Japanese affairs that marked increasing political effectiveness and a de facto modification of feudalism that was quite significant.

Cultural change accompanied this development, as well. Even though Japan's intense interactions with China were things of the past, the Japanese actually, during this early modern period, turned increasingly toward Confucianism. Buddhism survived and could be vigorous in some instances. The more traditional religion of Shintoism survived, as well, though it probably faded somewhat, but cultural emphases shifted increasingly to a Japanese version of Confucianism that had two consequences that would be significant for the future. Consequence number one was simply an increasing secularization of Japanese culture—not an entire secularization, but as Confucianism spread, this-worldly concerns began to predominate in Japanese culture, along, by the way, with some interesting new artistic forms that would mark further steps in Japanese cultural identity, as well.

The second implication of the Japanese version of Confucianism, though it became fully clear only in the first half of the 19th century, was an increasing commitment to the importance of education, not just for a Confucian upper class but for broader bands of society in what we would call the middle classes and even somewhat below. Japanese Confucianism ended up—not immediately but over time— encouraging an educational commitment that would lead Japan to be the second society after that of the West in literacy rates by the early 19th century. It's a very interesting pattern that, again, reflects considerable cultural dynamism in Japan itself.

These patterns in Japan obviously differed from those in other parts of East Asia, particularly China. The shogunate emphasized a growing importance of the central state, but feudalism was still quite real. The Japanese version of Confucianism was somewhat distinctive, particularly in its ultimate educational emphasis. Japanese population policy or Japanese population behavior was also somewhat distinctive during the 18th century. The Japanese population did not grow massively, did not overcome available resources, as was beginning to be suggested in China. The fairly extensive use of abortion, among other things, seems to have limited Japanese population growth. Most interesting of all for the future, the Japanese in the 18th century began to become slightly more open to outside influence rather than less. Decisions were made to exploit the contacts with Dutch merchants, and what was called the Dutch school of translators [was established] in Japan—people who learned Dutch in order to have the capability of interaction with Europeans. This contact was exploited to allow the translation of scientific and medical works into Japanese—not other works yet. This was an indication that the Japanese were sufficiently aware of what was going on in the outside world that they saw there was a need to take at least some opportunity to figure out what these developments might portend for Japan itself.

The patterns that we've been discussing don't overturn conventional views of Asian history in the early modern period entirely. Again, relative decline is undeniable, as long as it doesn't overwhelm an understanding that there were important positive developments during much of this period. Asia was not simply sitting around waiting for Western control and guidance. This was a series of independent kingdoms capable of significant achievements.

The specific decline of specific regimes, most notably in Mughal India, has to be registered, as well, but the larger sense that somehow this was a crucial period in which Asia began to be backward, isolated, or whatever the term is simply wrong. This leads to one final question: Why do we care? World historians—particularly experts on Asia and the world economy—have vigorously insisted that we need to redress this impression of Asian economic inferiority, backwardness, etc. I think the reasons are twofold. One is, presumably it's better to be accurate than not. When we have knowledge of things such as the Chinese acquisition of New World silver, we need to exploit it because otherwise we're simply pandering to error. I guess I would argue that, in itself, is a bad thing. Point two is we need to redress this impression because it also panders to older Western prejudices about Asian characteristics; it reflects a very brief sense of Western superiority. If we realize that Asia remained a vital contributor to world history up until at least the 18th and even into the 19th centuries and then would again become a vital contributor to world history by the 20th century, the period of Asian eclipse—if that's even an appropriate term—is very brief, indeed. This we have to know, whatever our views about historical accuracy, as a means of understanding Western Asian relations and Asian concerns about Western opinion, even in the present day.

Lecture Twenty-Four
The Long 19ᵗʰ Century

Scope:

World histories usually mark a new period in the later-18th century, contending that even though not all the themes are entirely new, there is enough change to warrant separate treatment. We look then to a period running from around the 1750s to World War I, which historian Eric Hobsbawm has dubbed "the Long 19th Century." This new period saw the decline or disappearance of most of the earlier land-based empires in favor of a simpler pattern of ascendant European imperialism. Europe's growing world dominance correspondingly redefined the world economy, which for a few decades balanced between a European (and U.S.) core and the peripheralization of almost every other region. The overwhelming new fact was the steadily growing manufacturing and military might of Europe, soon intensified by the results of the Industrial Revolution. Industrialization displaced much regional manufacturing in favor of European imports and generated changes in military technology that not only increased Europe's superiority on the seas but added ready dominance on land, as well. Around the edges of Europe's industrial dominance, two other themes began to emerge: first, a pattern of selective imitation of certain European developments that might be called the beginnings of modernization, copying elements of technology or education, for example, while retaining distinctive political forms; and second, the emergence of new levels of international connection under Western control that might be called a first stage of contemporary globalization.

Outline

I. The British historian Eric Hobsbawm called the period that runs from about 1750 to 1914 the Long 19th Century.

    A. Two features of the early modern period, the Colombian exchange and the land-based gunpowder empires, no longer had much impact in world affairs in the Long 19th Century.

    B. At the same time, two themes of the early modern period persist in this period.

1. The rise of the West, which continued and even accelerated compared to other societies.

2. The clearer shape of the world economy.

C. The two big developments that framed the Long 19th Century are the emergence of the Industrial Revolution and its brief but decisive monopoly by the West.

   1. The Industrial Revolution introduced a new economic form as decisively different from agriculture as agriculture was from hunting and gathering.

   2. Almost every aspect of life was touched by the Industrial Revolution as it began to take shape, first in Britain, then in other parts of Western Europe and the United States in the late-18th and early-19th centuries.

D. The Long 19th Century is also shaped by the extent to which Western societies monopolized the industrialization process. Ultimately, industrialization was a global phenomenon, but for the Long 19th Century itself, the enhancement of European power by industrialization set a framework to which every society had to react.

II. Even in its European monopoly, the Industrial Revolution was already, in crucial ways, global.

A. Europeans industrialized in part because they had already learned that an emphasis on producing processed goods was the way to make money in the world economy. Producing processed goods in factories simply enhanced and augmented that advantage.

B. Global relationships had also helped pile up capital in European coffers that was now available for investment in industrial apparatuses.

C. Industrialization had a global impact almost immediately, for example, in causing the deindustrialization of local industries in such places as India and Latin America.

   1. As British, European, and American factories poured out cheap manufactured goods, hundreds of thousands of domestic workers in Venezuela, India, and elsewhere were thrown out of work, forcing crucial economic adjustments in these regions.

III. Industrialization and European monopoly shaped the period in crucial respects.

    A. As Europe industrialized, it enhanced its demands on other parts of the world to produce cheap raw materials and foods and to accept manufactured products. In other words, it increased the extent to which core and peripheral or somewhat peripheral relationships began to predominate, not just in the Atlantic economy but worldwide.

        1. Latin America, for example, already a peripheral economy, saw more land and more workers devoted to production for export.

        2. Products here (such as silver, sugar, coffee, rubber, and fertilizer) still depended on low cost and yielded a modest profit to the society as a whole.

    B. As this relationship between Europe and other parts of the world was extended, the gap between core societies and peripheral societies widened as well.

    C. Africa was now deeply affected by the world economy.

        1. The slave trade was abolished in the 19th century, significantly limiting the principal African product in the world economy; yet African attachment to European goods continued, resulting in a scramble to identify other products that might sell in the world market, such as vegetable oil, palm oil, or cotton.

        2. These products, not always suitable to the African environment, required larger amounts of cheap labor, such that, ironically, slavery actually expanded in 19th-century Africa itself.

    D. Every part of the world was touched by this relationship, either becoming peripheral or expanding peripheral characteristics.

IV. Another consequence of this new pattern was an extension of European or Western military advantage from the seas to the land.

    A. Sea-based power was the dominant source of Western military threat in the early modern period, and it remained crucial.

B. However, a series of developments opened up the possibility of land-based military dominance. These innovations included the development of smaller, more mobile field artillery; the invention of the repeating rifle and the possibility of producing it on a mass scale; and the emergence of early forms of the machine gun.

C. Land-based military advantage was also enhanced by transportation improvements such as steamships and, in a few cases, railroads, along with the telegraph.

D. Finally, the development of new tropical medicines was an aid to Western military interaction in key parts of the world.

V. The new Western military edge was demonstrated in a series of major crises that quickly turned into larger patterns of economic exploitation.

    A. The first crisis took place in 1798, when Napoleon invaded and conquered Egypt.

        1. Although the British soon ousted the French, the ease with which European forces could conquer one of the heartland areas of the Islamic world was not lost on the Egyptians or the Ottomans.

        2. The balance between European military authority and Middle Eastern military power had been dramatically altered.

    B. The second crisis was the first Opium War in China in 1839, in which the British insisted that the Chinese accept opium (produced in British territories in India) and open their markets more generally.

        1. The Chinese government, weak now but still with some voice, resisted British demands.

        2. The result was a conflict in which British and other Western troops easily overcame Chinese forces and pried open the market for opium and for European and Western activities more generally.

    C. The third crisis took place in 1853, when an American fleet under Admiral Perry sailed into Ito Bay in Japan and demanded that the Japanese open their markets to Western goods.

  1. This was followed by another American expedition and a British expedition in 1854.

  2. The Japanese ultimately decided that they had no choice but to open their markets.

 D. The fourth crisis arose in 1854–1855, as the Russians were poised to seize additional Ottoman territory.

  1. Britain and France objected to Russian expansion and engaged Russia in the Crimea.

  2. Although the conflict was not easy, the West won again, and the power of industrial production, transportation, and technology applied to military activities made it clear that even Russia was behind.

 E. After these crises, there followed a series of military penetrations from the 1860s onward in Africa, some areas of the Pacific, and elsewhere.

 F. There were few parts of the world that Europe tried to enter militarily and failed. In most regions either direct military penetration or the threat of such penetration now reshaped the world to the West's advantage.

VI. The century of imperialism saw a simplification of the world economic patterns we have described previously. Two changes were crucial in this simplification:

 A. One, which we have touched on already, was the increasing exploitation of the bulk of the world by core societies, now including the United States.

 B. The second change was the effective elimination of externality. No major society could stay external because the West, through military pressure or economic cajoling, simply would not allow it.

VII. This new framework was an intensification of patterns that had been sketched, to some degree, in the early modern period, with the addition of two or three other components in the Long 19th Century.

 A. The early part of the Long 19th Century, in addition to being an age of early industrialization and imperialistic military activity, was also an age of Atlantic revolutions.

B. Beginning in the 1770s, a series of uprisings occurred in various parts of the Atlantic world, North America, Western Europe, and Latin America that would last through 1849.

    1. The ideological thrusts of these movements brought important political ideas onto the world stage, although many of the revolutionary ideals sincerely held by Europeans did not fit the relationships that Europe was forging in Asia and Africa.

    2. We see a lag between the emergence of revolutionary ideas and truly global impact. In the 20th century, however, reformers would use the ideologies of the revolutionary Atlantic world to spur national independence movements and social revolutions.

C. Another new global theme was the need for societies to decide how to respond to Western power. Should societies attempt to resist the West? What aspects of Western development could be imitated to regain or preserve some degree of regional independence?

    1. In the aftermath of Napoleon's invasions in Egypt, a new leader there, Muhammad Ali, undertook a path of reform that he hoped would bring industrialization and modern political and economic conditions to Egypt. Unfortunately, Western pressure and the limits of resources in Egypt tended to confine the durable results of Ali's reforms to the production of new cash crops that could serve the world market.

    2. Slightly later, the Ottoman Empire undertook reforms, with mixed results.

    3. Russia's reforms, beginning with the emancipation of the serfs in 1861, enabled that nation's participation in the industrialization process by the 1890s.

D. Western power affected different regions differently.

    1. Some areas, such as India and, increasingly, Africa, were held as outright colonies.

    2. Some areas, such as China, were simply targets of interference.

E. The responses of different regions varied. Even at the crest of European power we must look at world history in terms of interactions and not simply impositions.

VIII. A subordinate theme of the Long 19th Century was the tentative emergence of international institutions and arrangements that accompanied industrialization, and the increasingly global qualities of the world economy.

   A. Soon after the middle of the 19th century, for example, the Universal Postal Union was formed, as was the International Red Cross.

   B. Other international agreements allowed technological developments, such as the laying of undersea cables. Such agreements were Western dominated and, in one sense, a facet of imperialism itself, but they were also preliminary hints of a partial international political structure.

   C. International connections were furthered by the development of new transportation arrangements, including the cutting of the Suez and Panama canals.

   D. The 1880s saw the emergence of a series of private, international, nongovernmental organizations (NGOs) dealing with such issues as women's rights and white slavery.

IX. New patterns of cultural contacts are intriguing at the end of the Long 19th Century.

   A. The first sign of the potential for what we would now call a global consumer culture emerged in the final decade of the 19th century with the internationalization of several Western sports, including soccer and American baseball.

   B. This seemingly trivial development points to a final facet of the Long 19th Century: beneath the surface of exploitation and imperialism, new kinds of global connections and contacts were emerging. Some of these were institutional and some were evidence of international cultural interactions that help shape the next period in world history.

X. Let us close with a note on the brevity of the Long 19th Century.

   A. The Long 19th Century is a story of Western dominance, which makes this period, at least superficially, seem unusually simple.

B. The reason we end the period in 1914 is not only because that date marks the beginning of World War I, but also because, as a result of World War I, the easy Western dominance in the world began to come to an end.

Further Reading:

Peter N. Stearns, *The Industrial Revolution in World History* 3rd ed.

Timothy Parsons, *The British Imperial Century, 1815–1914.*

Shigeru Akita, ed., *Gentlemanly Capitalism, Imperialism and Global History.*

Questions to Consider:

1. Why was it difficult for non-European societies to match European economic and military achievements during the Long 19th Century? Why was it hard to industrialize?

2. If one compares India to the Ottoman Empire or China, was it more or less advantageous to be a European colony as opposed to a target of European interference during the 19th century?

Lecture Twenty-Four—Transcript
The Long 19ᵗʰ Century

In this session, we introduce the next major period in world history, which runs from about 1750–1914. The term that is increasingly used for this period is borrowed from a British historian, Eric Hobsbawm, the "Long 19th Century." Obviously, pretty long, but nevertheless focused on the 19th century. This period shades off from the early modern period in several ways—although as I mentioned before, there's no decisive break. In the first place, two of the features of the early modern period now no longer really have much effect in world affairs. The Colombian exchange had set up some enduring population patterns, but the immediate effects of the Colombian exchange are long gone by the later 18th century—except, again, in the Pacific region, where something of the same phenomenon was repeating itself. The formation of the gunpowder empires—at least, the land-based gunpowder empires—is also no longer a dominant theme. This is because—and this began to unravel in the late early modern period itself—many of the gunpowder empires are now in increasing trouble or vanishing altogether. So two early modern themes are pretty well gone.

On the other hand, two themes persist recognizably. One is the rise of the West, which continues and even accelerates vis-à-vis other societies in the Long 19th Century. [The second] is the shape of the world economy, which in fact, becomes clearer during this period, as well. This, then, is conventionally taken as a new period. I once tried to combine it with the early modern, but the conventions simply worked against it. It does have some new features, in addition to redefined continuities, from the early modern.

The two big developments—and they're closely linked—that framed the Long 19th Century, beginning in the later 18th century itself, are, one, the emergence of the Industrial Revolution and, two, its brief but decisive monopoly by the West. The Industrial Revolution is in and of itself a great big deal. It introduced a new economic form as decisively different from agriculture as agriculture was from hunting and gathering. With industrialization, human productive power increased vastly, primarily because of the use of fossil fuels and other sources of power than humans and animals. Industrialization was a big deal because it concentrated work and people in factories and cities. Not surprisingly, industrial societies fairly quickly—Britain was the first in 1850—reached a 50-percent mark of urbanization, which by the way, the world as a whole just reached in 2006, but an indication of the ongoing trend. The Industrial Revolution was a big deal because it transformed even intimate aspects of life—for example, childhood. Childhood in agricultural economies, as we emphasized, was mainly focused on work. Briefly, in the Industrial Revolution, that pattern might seem to continue, but pretty quickly it was realized that childhood and work in the factories did not mix. Childhood was redefined yet again as meaning primarily "schooling," something that we're still assimilating even today. Almost every aspect of life was touched by the Industrial Revolution as it began to take shape, first in Britain and then in other parts of Western Europe and the United States—late 18th, early 19th centuries—this does call attention to a major marker.

The second point is equally crucial. The Long 19th Century is shaped not only by the Industrial Revolution but by the extent to which, for a brief time, Western societies monopolized the process. Again, brevity is crucial here. Ultimately, it is absolutely vital to see the Industrial Revolution as a global phenomenon in which all parts of the world participate, such that the European lead is, again, a brief and, ultimately, probably not terribly significant one. For the Long 19th Century itself, the enhancement of European power by industrialization and by the fact that most other societies simply did not move immediately in an industrialization direction, this set a framework to which every society had, in one way or another, to react.

Even in its European monopoly, the Industrial Revolution was already, in crucial ways, global. It was caused in part by global connections. Europeans industrialized in part because they'd already learned that an emphasis on producing processed goods was a good way to make money in the world economy. Producing processed goods in factories simply enhanced and augmented that advantage. Global relationships also had helped pile up capital in European coffers that was available for the expensive—modest by contemporary standards but, by the standards of time, quite expensive—investments in industrial apparatus.

Industrialization also had a global impact immediately, for example, in causing the deindustrialization of local industries in places as different as India and Latin America. As British and European and American factories poured out cheap manufactured goods—particularly textiles—hundreds of thousands of domestic workers in places such as Venezuela or India were thrown out of work, obviously forcing crucial economic adjustments in these regions, as well as in the industrial societies themselves. Industrialization and European monopoly shape the period in crucial respects.

Two influences flow directly. In the first place, as Europe increasingly industrialized, it enhanced its demands on other parts of the world to produce cheap raw materials and foods and to accept increasingly expensive manufactured products—or, at least, increasingly available manufactured products. In other words, it increased the extent to which core and peripheral or somewhat peripheral relationships began to predominate, not just in the Atlantic economy, which really had been the main focus of the early modern period, but worldwide. Latin America, for example—and we'll explore this a little more fully in a later session—already a peripheral economy, saw more and more land and more and more workers poured into production for export. Now, these were not just of silver and sugar, though these continued, but also coffee, rubber, fertilizer, and a variety of products that still depended on low cost and yielded a fairly modest profit to the society as a whole, though still considerable wealth for individual businesspeople or landowners. This relationship, already established, was now vastly extended. As the relationship was extended, the gap between core societies and peripheral societies widened, as well. For example, in 1800, the average Mexican had a standard of living about two-thirds that of the average citizen of the new United States. In 1900, because the average American in a core society became wealthier and the average Mexican in a peripheral society became poorer, that relationship was one-third. It's a really significant change, reflecting movement in both directions.

Africa was now deeply affected by the world economy with an interesting and, in some ways, unexpected twist. The 19th century—and we'll explore this more fully in the next session—abolished the slave trade and significantly limited, therefore, the principal African sale to the world economy in the early modern period. Yet African attachment to the receipt of European goods—guns, etc.—continued, thus resulting in an African scramble to identify other products that might sell in the world market, such as vegetable oil, palm oil, or cotton. They were other products not always totally suitable to the African environment. They were products that also, again, demanded larger amounts of cheap labor, such that for a moment, ironically, slavery actually expanded in 19th-century Africa itself. Every part of the world was touched by this relationship, either becoming more peripheral in the first place or expanding peripheral characteristics, as was the pattern in Latin America. European and American thirst for cheap goods—ultimately, including even some cheap manufactured products—and their capacity to pay for these goods with an outpouring of manufactured products of their own set the world economic relationship into a global framework.

The second consequence of this new pattern—and it really does relate pretty closely to industrialization—was an extension of European or Western military advantage from the seas to the land, as well. Sea-based power remained crucial. This was the dominant source of Western military threat in the early modern period, and it obviously expands with better guns, larger ships, steamships, etc. Now, a series of developments also opened up the possibility of land-based military dominance, as well. These innovations included the development of smaller, more mobile field artillery, already used before industrialization outright—for example, by Napoleon in the French Revolutionary wars. The developments included the early-19th-century emergence of the repeating rifle and the possibility—which both British and American inventors helped to develop—of producing this repeating rifle through the standardization of parts on a mass scale. Developments included, by the middle of the century, the emergence of early forms of the machine gun—i.e., these developments made it possible for small numbers of Western troops, sometimes literally a few score, to hold off sometimes several thousands, even tens of thousands, of troops armed in more conventional fashion, as would occur in the European imperialist burst in Africa.

The land-based military advantage was enhanced, as well, by transportation improvements. Steamships and, in a few cases, railroads allowed Westerners to ship troops and material long distances in fairly rapid order. The telegraph, by providing communication links, contributed here. Riverboats, steam-driven, now could plow upriver, which was critically important for European military penetration in both China and Africa. Lastly, though more in the later 19th century, the development of new tropical medicines added another ingredient that facilitated Western military interaction with key parts of the world. Add these new things together and one has, first, a series of major crises in which the new Western military edge over other societies was demonstrated. They were crises that also quickly turned into larger patterns of economic exploitation, as well.

Event number one was in 1798. Napoleon, briefly freed from much to do back in Europe, takes a French expeditionary force and invades Egypt, conquering Egypt fairly easily. He doesn't stay there because the British chase him out, but the ease with which European forces could conquer one of the heartland areas of the Islamic world was not lost on Egyptians or on the Ottomans more generally. They didn't quite know what to do about it, but the balance between European military authority and Middle Eastern military power had clearly been dramatically altered.

Crisis number two was the first Opium War in China in 1839. The British, in the 1830s, found a good that they could produce quite easily, other than simply transporting New World silver that would get them access to Chinese markets. This good was opium, produced in British territories in India. The British insisted that the Chinese accept opium and open their markets more generally. The Chinese government, weak now but still with some voice, resisted British demands. The result was a conflict in which British and other Western troops easily overcame Chinese forces and pried open—at least, began to pry open—this market, both for opium, which was the widest-selling single good in the 19th-century world trade, and for European and Western activities more generally.

Crisis number three: In 1853, an American fleet under Admiral Perry sailed into Edo Bay in Japan—now Tokyo Bay—and demanded that the Japanese open their markets to Western goods. This was followed not only by another American expedition but by a British expedition in 1854. After considerable internal turmoil, the Japanese did indeed decide that they had no choice but to open. Indeed, in an unusually constructive reaction, it [the Western intrusion] would launch a process of reform that went well beyond simple response to Western demands.

Crisis number four was in 1854–55. The Russians had successfully achieved another territorial victory over the Ottomans and were poised to pry more Ottoman territory away. Britain and France objected for various reasons, including British fear about increasing Russian interference with British contacts with India. Britain and France went to war against Russia in the Crimea—essentially, literally, in Russia's backyard—and, although this was not an easy conflict, with many losses on both sides, the West won again. The power of industrial production, industrial transportation, and industrial technology applied to the military area now made it clear that even Russia was behind. Then there followed a series of military explosions and penetrations from the 1860s onward, particularly in Africa, also in additional areas of the Pacific, etc.

There were few parts of the world that Europe tried to enter militarily where it failed. The leading one, ironically, was Afghanistan. For most parts of the world, either direct military penetration or the successful threat of this penetration now reshaped the world—at least, again, briefly—to the West's advantage. This was, of course, the century of imperialism, a familiar label, but it can be taken even more deeply. What happened fundamentally was a simplification of the world economic patterns we've described previously. Two changes were crucial. One we've touched on already; that was the intensification of the exploitation of the bulk of the world—not now just parts of the world but the bulk of the world—by core societies, now increasingly including the United States. The second change—and here's where the military part comes in—was the effective elimination of externality. No major society could now stay external because the West, through military pressure if not economic cajoling, simply wouldn't allow it. Thus, societies that had regulated Western contacts previously, such as China, now found themselves incapable of maintaining this regulation. Societies that had sought partial isolation previously, such as Japan and Korea, now find that they are not allowed to do this either. With a very, very small number of exceptions, the world is open to the Western dominated world economy for a brief series of decades.

This framework really was, if you will, an intensification—a redefinition but intensification—of patterns that already had been sketched, to some degree, in the early modern period. In this framework, two or three other components get added in the Long

19th Century, which need attention, as well. First of all, this was, of course, at least the early part of the Long 19th Century, not only an age of early industrialization and its global impact, not only an age of new imperialistic military activities, but also an age of Atlantic revolutions.

Beginning in the 1770s, a series of risings occurred in various parts of the Atlantic world—in North America, in parts of Western Europe, and in Latin America—that would extend from the 1770s on to 1848–49, creating new political regimes [and] new attention to ideologies of liberty, legal and, possibly, even social and economic equality—a whole series of new ideological thrusts that brought important new political ideas and concrete illustration of those ideas onto the world stage. It isn't entirely easy to talk about how this other important initiative fully matches the larger framework that was shaped by industrialization and Western military dominance. This is because, frankly, many of the revolutionary ideals sincerely espoused by Europeans themselves didn't clearly fit the kinds of relationships that Europe was also forging with places in Asia and Africa. After all, if the new battle cry was freedom and political participation, imperialism was a denial of freedom—at least in many respects—and clearly, a denial of political participation. There was a long lag on a global basis between the emergence of new revolutionary thrusts and truly global impact.

Atlantic impact was quite clear, and this is an important aspect of the Long 19th Century, but global impact, in a way, would turn out to be greater in the 20th century than in the Long 19th. This is because it's in the 20th century that various kinds of revolutionaries and reformers would utilize the ideologies of the revolutionary West or the revolutionary Atlantic world to help spur national independence movements, social revolutions, and that sort of thing. This is a category of developments in the Long 19th Century. We don't want to forget about it, and we will indeed see one clear impact in our next discussion of slavery and abolitionism, but it doesn't totally fit the patterns that we're indicating.

Somewhat more general—and we will return to this one also in greater detail, but we can have a first stab at it now—was another new global theme. It has to be phrased carefully, but I think it's a valid one. Another new global theme was a need to figure out how to respond to the West. Western power, by the middle of the 19th

century, was so palpable and unavoidable that virtually every major society or some segment of it had to begin discussing: What are we going to do about it? How can we get rid of the West, resist the West, and what do we need to change in order to do so? What do we need to change that might imitate, at least, aspects of Western development itself for the opportunity to regain or preserve some degree of regional independence?

An early illustration of this new sense of a need to change in order to resist the West occurred in the aftermath of Napoleon's invasions. It occurred in Egypt, where a new leader in the 19th century, Muhammad Ali, effectively moved Egypt toward de facto independence from the Ottoman Empire. He undertook a path of reform that he hoped would bring industrialization and modern political and economic conditions to Egypt, allowing it to retain independence from the West, which was otherwise clearly threatened. Muhammad Ali sent scores of Egyptian students to European schools to learn engineering, modern science, and other technologies. He sought to encourage Egyptian industry. He sought to encourage new kinds of cash crops in Egyptian agriculture, such as cotton. It was an extremely interesting effort, but it was also extremely interesting that this early attempt largely failed. Western pressure and the limits of resources in Egypt itself tended to confine the durable results of this reform movement to the production of new cash crops that could serve the world market. Egyptian industrialization was not in the cards at this point, but again, it was a revealing episode.

Slightly later, the Ottoman Empire would undertake patterns of reform. It was seeking to redo its constitutional structure, to at least admit some new types of political institutions in the Western model, seeking to streamline its bureaucracy; seeking to create a more efficient, forward-looking bureaucracy; and seeking to improve and modernize its educational system. Again, these reform movements, which crested in the late 1830s and again in the 1870s, had mixed results. They were not ungenuine, but they obviously also did not move the Ottoman Empire to a position of reversing its pattern of difficulty in the face of Western interference and objections.

Russia would launch a major reform movement beginning with the emancipation of the serfs in 1861, leading not only to this emancipation but to significant new local political institutions. There were reforms of Russian law toward a reduction in the severity of punishments, codification of law, and efforts to spur industrialization. By the 1890s, Russia was indeed launched in a significant process. It was one of the first such processes to take hold outside of the West proper.

Reform, in other words, was in the air. However, this is where the complexity has to enter in. While I think it is fair to say that world history in the Long 19th Century—particularly, the second half of the Long 19th Century—is partly framed not just in terms of new Western industrial power and military interference but in terms of efforts at reform and reaction, it is important to recognize two things. First of all, Western power affected different regions differently. Some were held, such as India and, increasingly, Africa, as outright colonies. Some were simply targets of interference, such as China. People have debated whether it wasn't actually better for a while to be a colony than to be a target of external exploitation the way China was.

European contact varied; so did traditions and 19th-century conditions. Although this is not really totally predictable from earlier Chinese history, China responded slowly and long inadequately to the reform pressure. Only in the 1890s, does a real reform movement begin to catch hold in China. This is, again, partly because of traditional resentment of outside interference and models, partly because of the outside interference itself, and partly because Chinese governments, at this point, were exceptionally ineffective. It [Chinese government] was in one of those downward spins in the Chinese political process that occurred periodically. This was obviously quite a different response from that of Russia or Japan—a comparison that we'll take up a bit later—and even from the Ottoman Empire.

Responses varied, and it is vitally important to recognize this variety and recognize that, even at the crest of European power, world history needs to be seen in terms of interactions and not simply imposition. Nowhere, even in its darkest colonial holdings, did the West simply impose conditions on other societies. There were always reactions, always combinations, and always resistances. In this sense, the richness of world history, the need for comparison and variety, continues quite strong even in a century that, in broad outline, seems particularly simple—i.e., imperialism and European dominance.

One final facet of the Long 19th Century I think is worth mentioning, even though, frankly, it's a subordinate theme. That was the tentative emergence of new kinds of international institutions and arrangements that accompanied industrialization and the increasingly global qualities of the world economy. Let me mention a couple of particularly salient developments. It was soon after the middle of the 19th century, for example, that the Universal Postal Union was formed. It was a series of agreements dominated by Western players speaking on behalf of the whole world that allowed individual nations to agree on how to transmit mail from one society to the next. We now obviously pretty much take international postal service for granted, except in times of chaos or revolution, but it's really only in the later 19th century that this international facility came into being.

It was soon after the 1860s, as well, that the International Red Cross formed. Initially, again, it was a Western organization primarily, but one that began to help set standards not just for medical activities during wartime but for broader agreements that other societies would gradually adhere to. At least on paper, it sought to regulate some of the worst effects of modern war, particularly in areas such as treatment of the wounded and treatment of prisoners.

Other international agreements allowed, obviously, technological developments, such as the laying of undersea cables, etc. They were Western dominated in one sense, a facet of imperialism itself, the fact that international agreements were beginning to come into being—and one could mention also, at the very end of the 19th century, the emergence of a new world court in The Hague—but these developments were at least preliminary hints of a partial international political structure that was itself a marked innovation.

International connections were also furthered, of course, by the development of not only new technologies but of new transportation arrangements. The cutting of two great canals in the Long 19th Century—first, the Suez and, then, the Panama—were huge developments facilitating international contact and trade. This, obviously, fits the spread of the world economy model, but it deserves separate notice because, again, you're talking about new kinds of global connections that could go beyond trade.

The 1880s, again, toward the end of the Long 19th Century, saw the emergence of a new series of private international nongovernmental organizations. They were dealing with issues such as women's rights, white slavery, and problems of this sort. Again, we'll touch on some of this in our next session, as well. This first spate of what we would now call international NGOs was another sign that people—always first from the West because the West was the dominant player still—were beginning to think in terms of new kinds of international connections that would relate to the world economy but that would go well beyond it.

New patterns of cultural contacts are intriguing at the end of the Long 19th Century. The first real sign of a new potential for what we would now call a global consumer culture emerges in the final decade of the 19th century, in the beginnings of the internationalization of several key Western sports—most notably, from Britain, soccer, which begins to spread to Latin America, to parts of Asia, and by the 1920s, a little bit after our period, literally, the whole world. It was on its way to becoming the world's most agreed-upon international sport. Also in the late 19th century were the beginnings of the spread of American baseball to Latin America and the Caribbean, but also to Japan, Korea, and elsewhere. A Japanese baseball team defeated an American navy team in the mid-1890s, to the great delight of the Japanese. These developments, seemingly sort of trivial, are another sign of a final facet of the Long 19th Century that needs to be noted—beneath the surface of exploitation, imperialism, etc., is the beginning of the emergence of new kinds of global connections and contacts. Some of them were institutional; some of them, new evidences of international cultural interactions that would gain a life of their own and help shape the next period in world history, as well.

Let me emphasize, finally, the brevity of this Long 19th Century—particularly, the extent to which many crucial developments spread not just through the whole Long 19th Century but in its final half or two-thirds. This is a story of Western dominance. It is a story of Western economic and military controls that are striking, that make this period, at least superficially, unusually simple, but again, it's also brief. The reason we end the period in 1914—though we'll have to talk about this more in a subsequent discussion—is not just because of the dramatic fact of World War I, but because it was during and as a result of World War I that this kind of easy Western dominance in the world at large began to come to an end. These were a few decades that are very interesting and very important—we live with their legacy still—but a few decades only.

Biographical Notes

Alexander the Great (356–323 BCE): Successor of Philip II. He successfully conquered the Persian Empire before his death and attempted to combine Greek and Persian cultures.

Ban Chao (45–c. 115 CE): An influential female intellectual and writer in the Han dynasty. Her advice to women was republished in the 19th century.

Buddha (c. 6th century BCE): Creator of a major Indian and Asian religion; born as the son of a local ruler among Aryan tribes located near the Himalayas. He became an ascetic, found enlightenment under a bo tree, and taught that it could be achieved only by abandoning desires for all earthly things.

Chinggis Khan: Born in the 1170s, in the decades following the death of Kabul Khan, and elected khagan of all Mongol tribes in 1206, Chinggis Khan was responsible for the conquest of the northern kingdoms of China and territories as far west as the Abbasid regions. He died in 1227, before the conquest of more of the Islamic world.

Confucius (c. 551–479 BCE): Also known as Kung Fuzi; major Chinese philosopher and author of *The Analects*. His philosophy was based on the need for restoration of order through the advice of superior men to be found among the *shi*.

Mikhail G. Gorbachev (b. 1931): U.S.S.R. premier after 1985. He renewed attacks on Stalinism, urged reduction in nuclear armament, and proclaimed the policies of *glasnost* and *perestroika*.

Herodotus (484–425 BCE): Frequently identified as the "father of history," Herodotus was a 5th-century traveler who detailed the conflict between Greece and Persia in an assortment of stories called *The Histories*. *The Histories* exemplifies Herodotus's unbiased and methodical research and writing style, on which the discipline of history has been modeled.

Ibn Battuta (c. 1304–1378): Arab traveler who described African societies and cultures in his travel records.

Kublai Khan (1215–1294): Grandson of Chinggis Khan and commander of the Mongol forces responsible for the conquest of China. He became khagan in 1260 and established the Sinicized Mongol Yuan dynasty in China in 1271.

Lao Tzu (c. 6th century BCE): A major Chinese philosopher, Lao Tzu recommended retreat from society into nature. His philosophy held that individuals should seek to become attuned with the *dao*.

Mansa Musa (d. 1337): Ruler of the Mali Empire during its height, between 1312 and 1337. A devoted Muslim who built mosques throughout the empire, he sought to spread Islam by propelling its major city, Timbuktu, to global prominence.

Peter the Great (1672–1725): Son of Alexis Romanov and Russian ruler from 1689 to 1725. His reign saw the continued growth of absolutism and conquest, along with definite interest in changing selected aspects of the Russian economy and culture through imitations of Western European models.

James Harvey Robinson (1863–1936): An innovative historian of the Victorian era who taught at the University of Pennsylvania (1891–95) and Columbia University (1895–1919). Robinson pioneered the idea behind a new type of history that stressed the multidisciplinary progress of humanity. He also sponsored a new emphasis on Western civilization in American teaching. During his distinguished career, he was president of the American Historical Association.

Socrates (469–399 BCE): Athenian philosopher of the later-5th century BCE and tutor of Plato. He urged rational reflection of moral decisions and was condemned to death for corrupting the minds of the Athenian youth.

Arnold Toynbee (1889–1975): A British historian whose 12-volume analysis of the rise and fall of civilizations, *A Study of History* (1934–61), was a synthesis of world history—a meta-history based on universal rhythms of rise, flowering, and decline.

Zoroaster: An ancient Persian religious prophet who is thought to have lived around 1000 BC He was the founder of Zoroastrianism, a religion asserting that man had been given the power to choose between good and evil. Zoroastrianism became not only the national religion of the Sassanian Empire but also a driving force behind the entire Persian civilization. Following Alexander the Great's conquest, Zoroastrianism died out in Persia but found new life as the basis of the Parsi religion in India.

Notes